It's all about the beads!

It's all about the beads!

Barbara Case

David and Charles

Dedication

For David, Mum, Andrew and Theresa.

A DAVID & CHARLES BOOK
Copyright © David & Charles Limited 2006

David & Charles is an F+W Publications Inc. company
4700 East Galbraith Road
Cincinnati, OH 45236

First published in the UK in 2006

Text, project designs and illustrations copyright © Barbara Case 2006

A catalogue record for this book is available from the British Library.

ISBN-13: 978-0-7153-2284-0 paperback
ISBN-10: 0-7153-2284-2 paperback

Printed in China by SNP Leefung
for David & Charles
Brunel House   Newton Abbot   Devon

Commissioning Editor	Vivienne Wells
Editor	Jennifer Proverbs
Art Editor	Lisa Wyman
Senior Designer	Sarah Underhill
Production Controller	Ros Napper
Project Editor	Jo Richardson
Photographer	Karl Adamson

Visit our website at www.davidandcharles.co.uk

David & Charles books are available from all good bookshops;
alternatively you can contact our Orderline on 0870 9908222 or
write to us at FREEPOST EX2 110, D&C Direct, Newton Abbot,
TQ12 4ZZ (no stamp required UK only); US customers call
800-289-0963 and Canadian customers call 800-840-5220.

CONTENTS

INTRODUCTION

Precisely how old is this beading business? It seems no one knows for sure, but the earliest signs of Man's fascination for beaded or strung jewellery date back at least 75,000 years, a fact to which the recent find of a shell necklace in a long-forgotten African burial site bears testimony. So maybe this occupation is our earliest and most consistent industry, and one in which you, in taking up the hobby of beading, become a part. In seaside souvenir shops across the world, the ubiquitous shell necklace is still in evidence, and frequently not looking too different from its 75,000-year-old predecessor, although beads have largely superseded these calcareous marine homes as jewellery items.

It is easy to see how the desire for, and the creation of, beads came into being. Imagine those long ago days when there was so little with which to adorn the body, when coastal dwellers were very likely to have feasted on the easy pickings of seashore molluscs, and then picture the subsequent pile of waste shells. It is probable that, like us today, they would have been fascinated by the beauty of these leftovers and wanted to find a decorative use for them. However, to do so, it would first have been necessary to drill a hole. The 'drill' would almost certainly have been a shard of bone, which, although soft itself, would have been aided in the drilling process by the, initially accidental, supplement of a few grains of sand. The resulting pierced shells would have been suspended on strips of leather thong or twisted grass cord to form the earliest jewellery. Imagine next the find of a pebble

with a natural hole, such as we have all seen on the beach – a perfect addition to the necklace of shells! Then another pebble, just as desirable, but with an incomplete hole. This would have provided a challenge for our bead-making ancestors, although with a little persistence the shell-drilling technique would eventually have completed the hole to form our very first true bead. From this point on it is easy to picture how our ancestors used all sorts of materials, from amber and natural stone to nuts and seeds, to make beads with drilled holes. Today we use the same materials, but the invention of glass beads, about 4,500 years ago, changed everything, giving us the beginnings of the huge choice of bead that we now enjoy. Gradually, the importance of beads grew until they became the currency of trade between many nations and regular trade routes around the world were established.

Beads still travel all around the world, not now as a currency, but as desirable items for beaders everywhere to be exchanged for real money, featured in the pages of a catalogue or on the Internet. We are fortunate that we now have such ready access to the world's most beautiful beads, spread out before us for easy selection. When I first started stringing necklaces back in the 1970s, finding beads was a very hit-and-miss affair and my sources of supply, varying from haberdashery shops to bric-a-brac stalls, offered a limited choice. Twenty years later, when I began my bead jewellery and supply business, the acquisition of beads became much easier and it wasn't long before bead makers worldwide were plying me with their wares. The problem then was limiting my choice to a manageable level!

Now the range of beads on offer is even wider and includes some simply stunning examples of the bead-makers' skills, alongside the everyday beads that every necklace requires. In keeping with the trend for new and better beads, findings, threads and wires have also improved and the choice has increased enormously in recent times. And all this is available to anyone at just the tap of a computer key or the press of a telephone keypad.

Perhaps because of our long association with beads, most people find them almost instinctively appealing, a fact that is not simply a feminine peculiarity, as in recent years even the most masculine of young men have been seen wearing a beaded necklace or bracelet. Of course, for the most part it is women who wear jewellery and today, more than ever before, that jewellery is beaded, thus giving an opportunity to match colours and design to clothes. We all know that wearing a special accessory can, with the right choice, absolutely 'make' an outfit, and with such variety of colour, size and design of bead on offer, you can choose to make and wear something that is unique and perfect for the occasion.

So, now I am going to follow on from my previous book, *Making Beaded Jewellery*, with lots more irresistible beaded items and, like that book, this one will take you from the basics through to new designs that would not have been possible ten years ago. I will introduce you to a wide range of beautiful new beads and find uses for some of the antiques that may be gathering dust in your jewellery box. The projects vary from simple hatpins,

which take just minutes to make, to elaborate necklaces that, while time-consuming to thread, are worthy of heirloom status when completed. I also give you ideas for special gifts, widely appealing yet inexpensive jewellery for everyday wear, as well as fund-raising items suitable for sale at fairs and fêtes. Hopefully, by the time you have finished reading this introduction, you will be inspired not only to make the designs that follow, but also to adapt my designs to produce your own unique beaded items.

About this Book

In preparation for project-making, the front section of the book offers a concise guide to the items you will need to get started, including beads, findings, thread or wire and basic tools – pliers and scissors. The more specialist tools are also detailed, but as you read through the book, it will be apparent that you do not need everything listed for each project. The basic techniques on which all the projects are based are then set out in easy-to-follow, illustrated steps, to which you can refer whenever required. The projects are presented in thematic sections, focusing on particular types of bead, such as pearls, or other materials, for instance shell, or popular jewellery items – thong necklaces and charm bracelets, for example. At-a-glance information on ease of making, time to make and the length of the finished article will help you make your choice of appropriate project at any given time, and instructional diagrams demonstrate key stages of the method.

ALL ABOUT BEADS

Throughout the book I will tell you what type of beads are used for each project, so that if you wish you can follow the project exactly. However, bear in mind that you can achieve alternative results by making up my designs using a variety of other beads. For instance, you may find that the specific semi-precious stone used to make a particular necklace difficult to obtain, or you may want your necklace to be in another colour, in which case you can choose alternative natural stone, glass or even acrylic beads. So, don't let my designs limit your imagination, but instead use them as a base for your own creativity and then choose from the huge array of beads at your disposal. The following is a brief summary of the many different varieties of bead that are available.

Rocailles

These are also known as seed beads and they are made in different sizes that vary from approximately 1mm to 5mm. The choice of colour is vast, as is the finish, and these tiny essentials to the beader's palette may be found in clear coloured glass, 'silver'-lined, lustred, matt, AB-coated or metallic. They are usually made from glass, although it is now possible to find acrylic versions. Rocailles are never sold singly, but usually by weight or packet. Most are inexpensive, but some, especially those in gold metallic, are surprisingly pricey, due in this case to a real gold content in the colouring. I would recommend that every beader purchases a good range of these beads, as they are essential to most beading projects. I would also advise you to find some containers that will allow for compartmentalized storage and easy selection of these tiny items, because once they become mixed together, you will have a very long task ahead to sort them out again!

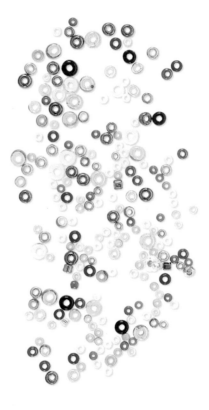

Bugles

These beads are similar to rocailles in that they are also sold by weight or packet, and are available in a wide range of colour and size. However, they differ in shape, being long, thin tubes of glass. Most are small, ranging from 2 x 5mm to 2 x 10mm, but there are some giant bugles to be found that can be 5 x 50mm in size. You will see bugles in use throughout the book. They are not quite as versatile as rocailles, but nevertheless they are extremely useful in many projects, and I find them especially appropriate for drop-style necklaces or earrings. The storage precautions mentioned above for rocailles also apply to bugles.

Larger Glass Beads

You will not be able to turn many pages of this book before you grasp the enormous variety of large glass beads that are available. Many countries are involved in their manufacture and in the average bead catalogue you are likely to find examples from India, Japan, Czech Republic, Austria, Ghana, Italy and Britain, as well as very individual items made by various glass artists. Quality varies from charming but crude beads, formed from recycled bottle glass in Ghana, to the exquisite perfection of cut crystal from Austria. Shape and size too is very variable and you will find anything from tiny to huge. The other obvious variation is in design, and while some beads may be very simple with perhaps just two colours, others may have a 'silver' or 'gold' foil core and an intricate surface pattern of many colours. The quality of lamp beads (see below) varies from country to country, with Japan, Czech Republic, China and Italy producing some of the finest, but those produced by the glass artists of Murano in Venice have been renowned for their excellence for many centuries.

Glass Bead Production

Many glass beads are mass produced, usually identifiable by a uniform appearance and a seam running around the middle or from top to bottom. Others are individual and painstakingly crafted. In India, the bead-making tradition is passed down through family generations. Heat to melt the glass is provided by simple lamp flames that are intensified by air blown from foot-operated bellows – hence the resulting beads being called lamp beads. Often, superficial coloured patterns are formed by trailing molten glass over the raw bead, each colour applied separately. Other glass bead makers employ more modern but essentially similar techniques.

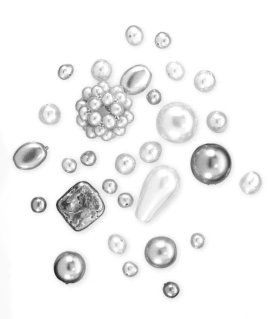

Pearls

Of all the advances in beads, perhaps pearls have made the biggest strides, and whereas once even cultured pearls were considered the prerogative of the wealthy, now we have an abundance of their freshwater cousins. Modern methods of culture provide us with a stunning range of colours, shapes and sizes, and all affordable for everyone. Of course, they are still not the cheapest of beads, but then neither are they the most expensive, and when you see the range that is on offer, you will not be able to resist their lustrous allure. As well as the beautiful cultured pearl, there are also artificial pearls. Plastic pearls, usually the least expensive, are lightweight, making them eminently suitable for stitching, and are used extensively for wedding dresses and veils. Glass pearls are more suitable for jewellery making and are available in a myriad of colours and sizes. Most glass pearls are made in the Czech Republic as well as Austria, where the famous Swarovski company manufacture them to a very high standard, and are a less-expensive alternative to real pearls.

Metal Beads

Like glass beads, metal ones are available in a huge variety, from plain 2mm base-metal rounds, through large intricately worked silver, to exquisite cloisonné and enamel. The Chinese are acknowledged experts in cloisonné and enamel work, and the resulting beads are simply beautiful. Almost invariably, metal beads are mixed with other bead types within a jewellery design and it is unusual to see a necklace that doesn't include just a few metal beads to give a lift to the colours of the others. The materials that are used in their manufacture also vary and you will come across beads made from brass, plated base metals, gold, silver, plated pewter and even metalized plastic. The latter have a plastic or acrylic base and a surface coating of a gold or silver colour. These beads are very useful, as they usually hold their colour well and are light in weight and also inexpensive.

Acrylics, Resins and Plastic

These are types of bead that until recent years I rather disliked, but now they have come of age and some acrylic beads really are most attractive. Often they look very much like glass, but some designs create a look that would be impossible to achieve in another material. At the bottom end of the range are beads aimed at children, which can be very useful if you are, for instance, producing items for a school fund-raising event. At the top end are gorgeous Italian beads, which appeal to more sophisticated tastes.

Ceramics

Even older than glass beads, ceramics have been around for many thousands of years, and it was the glazing of ceramic beads to produce the blue and green faience beads worn by Egyptian Pharaohs that eventually led to the production of glass beads. In more recent times, ceramic beads have been produced in a wide variety of designs, from the unpainted primitive terracottas of Africa to the finely painted porcelain of China.

Bone, Horn and Wood

Beads made from these natural sources have been around for as long as Man has been beading and there is a wide range of styles available to us, from the simple coloured wooden beads of childhood to intricately handcrafted carved bone. Many of the styles of jewellery made today and contained within this book would lend themselves to the use of this type of bead, but the contemporary trend is towards a lighter look, so here I have concentrated more on other beads. However, don't forget that any of these designs can be adapted to use this type of bead.

Semi-precious Stone

Perhaps no other type of bead captures the imagination in the same way as do those made from semi-precious stone. There is something quite enchanting about a material that is hewn from our Earth and far older than our historical records. Most people imagine that semi-precious stone beads are expensive, but in general this is not the case. Of course, you can expect to pay hundreds of pounds for a necklace length of rubies, emeralds or fine opals, but most of the more common stones, such as jaspers or quartzes, are inexpensive.

Other Beads

Anyone who becomes really interested in beads will soon discover that there are more types available than those previously mentioned. For instance, you will find examples in polymer clay, seeds, natural resins or shell.

MATERIALS

In addition to beads, you will need a range of the more basic materials for making up your designs into finished items, such as findings, thread and wire. The following is a brief guide to what is on offer.

Findings

Findings are the metal components that we need to complete nearly every piece of jewellery. From the clasp to finish a necklace, to the hook from which to hang an earring, they are the essential nuts and bolts that make jewellery work. In recent years, findings have kept pace with the demand for more sophisticated jewellery, and although the simple and inexpensive basics are still available and just as useful as ever, it is now easy, for instance, to find a clasp to match the quality and beauty of the beads in a special necklace, or to choose other components to enhance each item that you make. In the book, you will see a wide variety in use, matched to a suitable project.

Worthy of special mention are the niobium ear-hooks, which have appeared on the jewellery scene in recent years, and their colourful anodized finish is a real asset to anyone who loves earrings. And for those with allergies, the choice of niobium is most appropriate as it is highly unlikely to cause any adverse skin reaction. Another advantage of these ear-wires is that they are available unmade (straight-leg), i.e. the loop is unformed and the jewellery maker is able to choose beads that sit above the loop to match the drop beads.

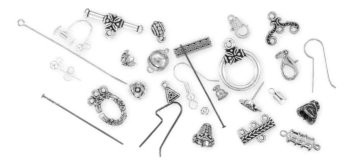

Allergies

Many people will be aware that nickel, which has been used in the manufacture of jewellery findings for many years, can cause allergic reactions. Consequently, in recent times the EU brought in a directive that reduced the amount of nickel permitted in such products to minute proportions and disallowed the sale of jewellery containing higher nickel content. However, not all countries adhere to these restrictions, and in the USA, for instance, nickel is still used in some jewellery metals. If you buy products made in a non-EU country, you should check out the nickel content before making your purchase.

Threads and Wires

One of the biggest advances in beading has been the innovation in the materials on which beads may be strung. When I first started beading, the best I could find was sewing thread, but now the beader is spoilt for choice, as you will see from the following, and that choice enables the beader to give free reign to their imagination. Throughout the book you will see all these different threads and wires 'in action'.

Threads

These are now available in various materials, from the strong and man-made materials to the traditional silk, and all are obtainable in a wide range of colours and varying thicknesses. Also, probably just about acceptable under the term of thread, we have clear nylon, which has provided the beader with the ideal medium with which to make the popular 'floating' bead necklace, as well as Stretch Magic, which looks a little similar to nylon but has a strong stretching ability, making it the ideal choice for claspless bracelets and children's necklaces.

Cord and Thong

Not many years ago there was just a simple choice to be made when choosing one of these materials – black or coloured leather or black thong – but now there is a wide choice of coloured waxed cotton. In addition, there is rat-tail, a silky cord that is made in a myriad of different colours, and some that, along a metre or yard length, exhibit several merged colours in rainbow, autumn or pastel shades. The more adventurous might like to seek out haberdashery shops or suppliers to find cords designed for purposes other than beading, or even make their own cord with such materials as coloured embroidery cottons (floss) by plaiting various colours or twisting the threads together. A special tool that looks like a carpenter's brace, called a spinster tool (see page 15), is available to make this latter task easier.

Wires

For the inventive beader, the recently developed, wonderfully colourful wires offer much scope for creativity, and they can be used to make highly individual pieces of jewellery. In many instances, these wires are simply colour-coated copper, but anodized niobium is now available for producing upmarket jewellery. This expensive material is suitable for those who suffer from skin allergies, and can be used to make beautiful long-lasting jewellery of superior quality.

Memory wire is a useful material for making simple jewellery. It is made in long coils of hard wire in three different diameters/lengths suitable for choker necklaces, bracelets and rings respectively. As its name suggests, it remembers its shape, so that when you pull it apart to thread beads or to wear, it springs back to a round and needs no clasp to fasten in place.

Nylon-coated Wires

Again, not so long ago, the only nylon-coated wire to be found was a rather stiff 'tiger-tail' in just one colour, 'silver'. This was, and still is, useful as a very strong, cheap wire 'thread' on which to suspend heavy beads, but it has a tendency to kink and hang stiffly when used with lighter beads.

Today, advances in manufacture have brought us beading wires that are even stronger, with up to 49 very fine wires in seven twisted bundles of seven beneath a smooth flexible coating of nylon. These wires have none of the previous kinking problems and are available in a wide range of colours, although in use, unless you wish the wire 'thread' to be seen, there is no need to use the coloured versions. This new wire really is superb; it is strong, flexible, adaptable and very easy to use. The two brands with which I am most familiar are Softflex and Beadalon, and I have used both of these throughout the book, so when I mention or list 'nylon-coated wire', it is one or other of these two.

Gimp

This is a very fine, flexible tube of coiled metal wire through which thread is passed where it is attached to the clasp, to give a neat, professional finish. It was once used mainly for pearl necklaces and so appeared only in 'gold' or 'silver'. These are still the most useful colours, but many other colours, as well as sizes, are available and it is possible to match the colour of gimp to your beads. Be careful how you store gimp, as it easily tangles and is very susceptible to being crushed due to the delicate nature of the wire.

TOOLS

To begin beading, and to make up the projects in this book, you will need the few basic items listed in the Basic Tool Kit below. However, as you become involved with this fascinating hobby, you will eventually want to purchase more specialist tools that make the tasks involved easier to carry out and to achieve more professional results.

Basic Tool Kit

You will require the following for completing each project in the book. Therefore, only the more specialist tools are itemized within each project.

- pair of cutting, round- and flat-nosed pliers, or a pair of general-purpose pliers, preferably the small beading variety (see below), but ordinary household pliers are acceptable

- sharp pair of scissors

- beading tray or household tray with separate shallow containers

Pliers

The main specialist tools for making jewellery are pliers and these come in a variety of types. They also vary in quality, the best being manufactured in Germany, and although relatively expensive, they should last a lifetime (my own pliers are nearly 30 years old!). But those costing less than half the price do the same job and are perfectly serviceable.

General-purpose Beading Pliers

In effect, these are a miniature version of household pliers, but their small size provides for greater dexterity. You can use them to do all the jobs that are required in beading, but more specialist pliers, such as those on the right, are very helpful.

Round-nosed Pliers

The sole purpose of round-nosed pliers is to aid in the smooth bending of wire and they are invaluable for anyone who intends to make a lot of earrings.

Flat- or Snipe-nosed Pliers

These are used for the most delicate jobs. They are similar to general-purpose pliers, but without the cutting facility and with a slightly smaller 'nose'. In practice, however, there are few beading jobs that cannot be done with a small pair of general-purpose pliers. So, if you are purchasing beading tools on a budget, this is the pair of pliers that is not essential.

Cutting Pliers

A pair of general-purpose pliers provides a cutting facility, but they are only of real use when dealing with straight wire. When you require greater accuracy or to cut in an area that is not easy to access, a pair of cutting pliers is essential.

Crimp Pliers

With the advent of a wider choice and better quality of nylon-coated wire, crimp beads, which are used to secure the wire onto a clasp, have also improved in quality, and whereas general-purpose pliers would once have been used to squeeze a base metal crimp bead flat onto the wire, crimp pliers to be used with special crimp beads are now available to do the job in much more stylish fashion. You will see many examples of their use later in the book.

Bead Reamer

This is an extremely useful tool for all beaders, but especially for those who frequently use semi-precious stone, which is hand-drilled. Nearly everyone who has done some beading will have come across that one bead (typically one of the last to be threaded) that has a malformed hole, through which it is impossible to pass the thread. Rather

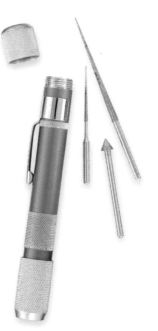

than frustratingly having to discard the bead, you can use a bead reamer to enlarge the existing hole. The tool is a hand-held tube in which are stored three different sizes and shapes of round file. At one end of the tube is a small chuck into which the required file is fitted to enable the easy enlargement of most bead holes. This tool will eventually pay for itself in salvaged beads.

Spinster Tool

This mini carpenter's brace look-alike is a useful tool for those who wish to make their own cord, as it speeds up the process of twisting threads to form a 'rope'.

Beading Trays

There is no doubt that you can easily work at beading using a domestic tray and several small flat containers to hold your beads (I find the flat, round lids that come with tubes of savoury snacks to be perfect!), and in some ways it can be preferable to a purpose-built tray, which gives you less space. However, a beading tray comes into its own when designing necklaces, as the beads can be laid in proposed order of threading within the specially designed necklace-shaped grooves. If you are a television beader, and like to pursue your hobby while sitting in your armchair, a lap tray with a bean-bag base would also be very useful.

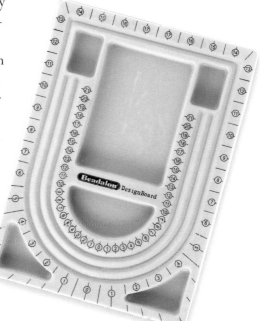

Storage

This is a vital consideration for all bead jewellery makers, and if you need to store a fairly large amount of beads, you need to find a system that suits your needs and your available space. I use a combination of small plastic 'chests of drawers' and other compartmentalized plastic boxes. However, a brief search through a few bead catalogues will reveal a wide array of variations on the same theme from which you can make your choice. Alternatively, most DIY stores supply plastic boxes and other storage items that are designed for the hobbyist in general, but are eminently suitable for the storage of beads and findings.

BASIC TECHNIQUES

There are a great many different techniques involved in bead jewellery making, but rather than demonstrating all of these in one go, in this section I will show you only the basics, to which you will find references throughout the book. These few easy techniques will give you the skills required to string two styles of simple necklace and make a pair of earrings.

Easy Start

The projects in the book are not overall presented in order of difficulty. However, the first two projects feature the simplest method of necklace and earring making, and even if you succeed only in making these items, you will have acquired a skill that will, at best, give you hours of crafting pleasure and, at worst, the ability to re-string most broken necklaces.

Simple Necklace Stringing

Nylon-coated wire is suitable for stringing most necklaces. It is flexible enough for all but the lightest of beads to hang well and is made in three different diameters, which, for simplicity's sake, I will refer to as fine, medium and thick. The medium-thickness wire is the best for most projects. Later in the book I cover other threading mediums and techniques, including knotting with beading thread (see pages 57–58).

Many large beads are handmade and usually this means that they are not uniform in size. Therefore, when designing your necklace, look carefully at your beads and be careful to use the different sizes accordingly, i.e. in most designs the larger beads should be kept for the front of the necklace, with the smaller ones being set close to the clasp at the back. For the purposes of instruction, I am assuming that we are stringing plain beads.

INGREDIENTS ◎ beads ◎ 2 crimp beads ◎ gimp (optional – see Step 3) ◎ 1 clasp ◎ length of nylon-coated wire, about 100mm (4in) longer than the proposed necklace ◎ beading tray or household tray with separate shallow containers ◎ pair of cutting pliers ◎ pair of flat-nosed or general-purpose pliers, or a pair of crimp pliers

1 Assemble all your components on a beading tray or a household tray with separate shallow containers.

2 Thread one crimp bead onto one end of the nylon-coated wire.

3 With your cutting pliers, cut two 8mm (^{3}/$_8$in) lengths of gimp and then thread one length onto the same end of the nylon-coated wire (diagram A). It is not essential to use gimp, but its use does give a professional appearance to the finished item. You will see examples of necklaces made both with and without gimp throughout the book.

A

4 Thread on the clasp and then thread the long end of the wire back through the crimp bead to form a loop (diagrams B and C).

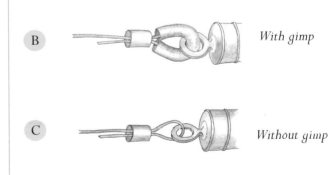

B   *With gimp*

C   *Without gimp*

Crimp Beads

There are two types of crimp bead. The cheaper version is applied by using a pair of general-purpose pliers, but the more expensive goldfill or sterling silver versions are best applied with a purpose-made pair of crimp pliers (see page 14 and Step 5 below). There is no need to use much force when using either type of crimp, as it is only necessary for it to 'bite' into the wire a little to secure it. However, before proceeding, make sure that it is secure on the wire.

5 *For inexpensive crimps,* use flat-nosed or general-purpose pliers to squeeze the crimp bead onto the nylon-coated wire (diagrams D and E). For clarity, the nylon-coated wire is not shown in the diagrams.

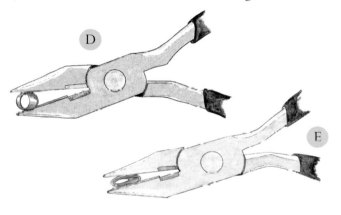

For best-quality crimps, use a pair of crimp pliers, which has two sets of grooves in its 'jaws' and applies the crimp in a two-stage process. First, place the crimp into groove (a) and squeeze. Then, place it into groove (b) and squeeze the pliers again – this has the effect of rounding the crimp (diagrams F–H). Again, for clarity, the nylon-coated wire is not shown in the diagrams.

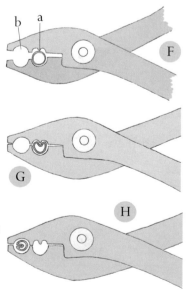

6 Thread beads onto the nylon-coated wire and, if possible, slide them over the short end of the wire near the crimp so that it is hidden beneath the beads. Sometimes, due to the small holes in beads, this is not possible, and providing the crimp bead is secure, it is safe to use your cutting pliers to trim the wire close to the crimp (diagram I).

7 When all beads have been threaded on, hold your necklace up by the unthreaded end of the wire and allow the weight of the beads to take up the slack in the thread (diagram J).

8 Thread the remaining crimp bead onto the free end of the nylon-coated wire, then thread on the other length of gimp, if using, as in Step 3. Thread the wire through the clasp as in Step 4, then secure the crimp following the appropriate method in Step 5 and trim the wire, as in Step 6.

Safety for Children

It is advisable that older children are supervised until they become competent at handling beading tools and sharp wire, etc. As well as these tools and materials, beads should be kept out of the reach of young children at all times.

Making a Thong Necklace

The earliest necklaces in history were strung either on a leather or twisted grass thong. There are various styles of necklace end available for use with thong, but all work on a similar principle, i.e. they cover the end of the thong and are secured in place by being squeezed with pliers. Here, I demonstrate the use of a square calotte crimp, which is suitable for all types of thong, such as leather, suede, cotton cord, rat-tail, ribbon and handmade cords.

INGREDIENTS ◎ beads ◎ 2 jump rings (not always needed, as seen in some projects) ◎ 2 square calotte crimps ◎ 1 clasp ◎ length of cord or thong to suit your requirements ◎ beading tray or household tray with separate shallow containers ◎ pair of flat-nosed or general-purpose pliers

1 Assemble all your components on a beading tray or household tray with separate shallow containers.

2 Cut the end of the cord or thong square and place it in one of the calotte crimps.

3 Use flat-nosed or general-purpose pliers to bend first one side of the calotte crimp and then the other side over and down onto the thong (diagram A).

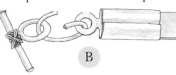

A

4 Use your pliers to open one jump ring sideways (if possible, never pull a jump ring or any other wire loop apart at the joint, as this weakens the link). Thread the jump ring through the loop of the calotte crimp, then thread on one part of your clasp (diagram B).

B

5 Use your pliers to close the jump ring and secure your clasp to the end of the thong. Now thread your beads onto the cord or thong. Optionally, you can ensure that they sit centrally by tying an overhand knot in the thong at either side of the threaded beads; otherwise, they can remain loose.

6 When you are satisfied with the arrangement of your threaded beads, complete the necklace by attaching the remaining calotte crimp and the other part of the clasp to the other end of the cord or thong, as in Steps 2–5.

Basic Earring Making

There is no mystery to earring making and most beaded designs are based on threading beads onto headpins and simply bending wires to form loops for linking beaded headpins together. However, some people do find forming perfect loops in wire a challenge, and for that reason I grade most earrings with a 3 for ease of making. But don't be put off – it really is just a matter of practice and soon you will be creating your own stunning ear adornments!

INGREDIENTS ◎ beads ◎ 2 headpins (normally 50mm, although other sizes are available) ◎ 2 ready-made ear-hooks, ear-studs or ear-clips ◎ beading tray or household tray with separate shallow containers ◎ pair of flat-nosed, cutting and round-nosed pliers (it is possible to make a pair of earrings using a pair of general-purpose pliers, but it will be more difficult to form a good loop)

1 Assemble all your components on a beading tray or household tray with separate shallow containers.

2 Select your beads and thread them onto a headpin (diagram A).

3 Use flat-nosed pliers to bend the wire over at a right angle close to the top bead (diagram B).

4 Use the cutting pliers to trim the excess wire, leaving 8–10mm (less than ½in) (diagram C)

5 Use the round-nosed pliers to form a loop. For best results, do this gradually rather than in a single motion (diagrams D and E).

6 To finish, attach the drop to the loop of your chosen ear-fitting by opening the loop made in Step 5 sideways (as for a jump ring – see left). Repeat Steps 2–6 using the other headpin to make a matching earring.

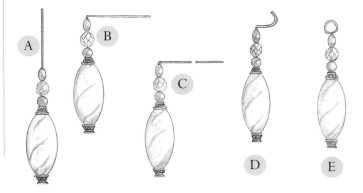

A   B   C   D   E

Tailor-making Ear-hooks

Alternatively, you can make straight-leg ear-hooks, which provide the opportunity to coordinate the ear-hook with the drop, as you will see in several projects throughout the book. Thread one or two small beads onto the 'leg' of the ear-hook, making sure that there is enough spare wire to form a loop (diagrams A and B). Follow Steps 3 and 5 opposite to form a loop, then attach the finished ear-hook to the drop.

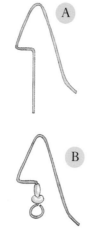

Using Larger-holed Beads

Sometimes, the main beads you wish to use have just too large a hole to either be held by, or sit straight on, the headpin or, in the case of a necklace, on the thread. But don't worry, this problem is easily overcome. First, thread onto your headpin or length of thread a bead or bead cap that will not slide inside the main bead, then simply use smaller beads, such as rocailles or bugles (see page 8), to thread onto the headpin or thread and inside the main bead (diagram A). When the hole of the main bead is full, thread on another larger bead, or bead cap, to hold it in place (diagram B). You can then continue to thread on beads as normal.

Niobium

If your headpins or ear-hooks are made from niobium, you should cover the jaws of the pliers with clear adhesive tape to protect the anodized colour finish. This applies to all work with niobium, as although the finish is durable in normal wear, it is easily scratched.

About the Projects

Each project is presented in 'recipe'-style format, with a list of 'ingredients' itemizing the type and quantity of beads, threads and so on required in detail, together with a step-by-step method. Although these materials can be varied and adapted to suit your taste and preference, it is a good idea to begin by following a few of the simpler projects exactly, in order to build your skills and confidence.

Which Project?

To help you decide which projects you are ready to tackle, I grade them on a scale of 1 to 10, with 1 being the simplest and 10 being the most complex. I also give an approximate length of time that you, as a novice beader, might expect to take to make the item.

I have opted to use the best-quality 'ingredients' available, because I believe that if you are to invest time and effort in a project, it should look good for many years to come. Therefore, the featured beads and findings tend to be a little more expensive than is strictly necessary, so if your budget is limited, you can choose cheaper alternatives, which are readily available.

Reading the Recipes

Do bear in mind the following points when you come to the individual projects:

◎ If just 'bead' is listed in the ingredients, you should assume this to be round; all other shapes/types are specifically described, e.g. oval or rocaille.

◎ Where rocailles or bugles are listed in the ingredients, I usually do not specify an amount, since these small beads are always purchased by weight or by the packet.

◎ Where metal items are specified as 'gold' or 'silver', i.e. within quotation marks, this indicates that they are imitation.

◎ Wherever reference is made to thread or threading in a recipe method, this means the specific type of threading medium listed in the ingredients, e.g. wire, nylon-coated wire, monofilament nylon, cord, thong, ribbon, etc.

◎ You can assume that the width of the threading medium required is medium, unless otherwise stated.

◎ Equivalent imperial measurements for metric are normally given to the nearest ¼in, although for some larger measurements, the imperial figure is rounded up or down.

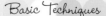

MEMORY LANE

Most of my own best-loved necklaces are those made from old beads. Some are unusual or rare, but others are simply beautiful. Many of us keep old and broken necklaces because the beads are too lovely to throw away, so search your jewellery or junk boxes for forgotten riches, or visit a few antique fairs or shops. Sometimes you may find only one or a few beads of a type, so a little thought is needed to make the most of what you have. For instance, a striking large bead may, with the addition of very few others, make a stunning pendant, or, with carefully chosen new beads, become the focus for a truly unique item of jewellery.

A few of my own prized finds shown here include a centuries-old, silver-capped carnelian bead, originating from Turkmenistan, worn smooth with age and yak grease. The decorative yellow beads are from the famous Gablonez factory in the Czech Republic and the perfect black and white millefiore from the Moretti & f.lli bead makers in Murano, Venice. Once you start looking, you could find yourself addicted to the special lure of old beads!

Junk Box Gems

—Ease of making: 1
—Time to make: 45 minutes
—Length: 410mm (16¼in)

This starter project makes creative use of any old beads that you may have uncovered in your searches through your jewellery and junk boxes, or from other likely sources. Here, I selected the main beads and rocailles from an ancient hoard given to me by friends, to which I added some new items such as the bead caps and the blue/gold medium-sized beads in the supporting role. These were purchased from a US supplier, Jewelex (see page 126), which has a large stock of old but unused quality beads.

The large blue/yellow millefiore beads are Venetian (probably around 70 years old), and the smaller 11mm blue/gold beads are either Czech or Japanese. The gold sparkle in these is created by the inclusion of aventurine glass, which incorporates fine copper 'dust'.

The clasp and bead caps are from one of my favourite manufacturers, Tierracast (see page 126), which produces fine-quality pewter castings that are available plated in 22ct gold, Fine Silver, Copper or Rhodium.

The ingredients below are for the necklace; see over the page for how to make the matching earrings.

INGREDIENTS

◎ 9 round old millefiore beads, 15mm
◎ 10 blue/gold round beads, 11mm
◎ 2 blue faceted round beads, 4mm
◎ 18 gold-plated bead caps, 12mm
◎ 24 gold-plated bead caps, 4mm
◎ 20 small yellow rocailles
◎ 2 goldfill crimp beads
◎ 2 x 8mm (³/₈in) lengths of 'gold' gimp
◎ 1 gold-plated toggle clasp
◎ 500mm (20in) length of nylon-coated wire

To make up the necklace, refer to the photograph for the threading sequence and follow the instructions for Simple Necklace Stringing, page 16.

Attic Earrings

- Ease of making: 3
- Time to make: 10 minutes
- Length: 50mm (2in)

Very often when using old beads there will simply not be enough to make anything other than a pair of earrings, or you may have just a few left over after making a necklace. I was left with just two of the blue/gold beads when making the preceding project, so I used these to make the pair of matching earrings shown here. The other two pairs of earrings shown on the previous page were made in the same way from old Venetian beads. The main beads for the black earrings date from around 1820; the creamy coloured ones are about 100 years younger.

INGREDIENTS

- ◎ 2 blue/gold round beads, 11mm
- ◎ 2 blue faceted round beads, 4mm
- ◎ 6 small yellow rocailles
- ◎ 2 goldfill oval beads, 2 x 4mm
- ◎ 8 gold-plated bead caps, 4mm
- ◎ 2 blue anodized niobium headpins, 50mm
- ◎ 2 blue anodized niobium straight-leg angular ear-hooks

To make up the earrings, refer to the photograph on page 21 for the threading sequence and follow the instructions for Basic Earring Making, page 18.

Singing the Blues

- Ease of making: 6
- Time to make: 3 hours
- Length: 200mm (8in)

Just because I have graded this bracelet 6 in difficulty doesn't mean you should look for an easier project! The main task is still simple stringing, but you do need dexterity and to be careful when counting beads.

The main beads in this striking bracelet are probably Japanese. They are old, but until now unused, and from the same source as the blue/gold beads in the previous project. This shape and type of bead is often found in old necklaces, and also similar beads can be obtained from suppliers of new beads. The frosted appearance of the new 4mm beads provides a perfect foil for the bluebell sheen of their larger cousins.

The clasp for a bracelet needs to be easy to close and open with one hand, and the toggle clasp I have used here is ideal. Measure the wrist of the person for whom the bracelet is intended, as you may have to adjust the length.

INGREDIENTS

- ◎ 10 blue flat oval beads, 12 x 18mm
- ◎ 22 frosted blue beads, 4mm
- ◎ 20 gold-plated beaded rondels, 4mm
- ◎ blue AB-coated rocailles
- ◎ 2 'gold' jump rings
- ◎ 6 goldfill crimp beads
- ◎ 3 inexpensive crimp beads for use as temporary 'stoppers'
- ◎ 2 gold-plated 3–1 necklace/ bracelet ends
- ◎ 1 gold-plated toggle clasp
- ◎ 2 x 25mm (1in) lengths of nylon-coated wire
- ◎ 2 x 60mm (2½in) lengths of nylon-coated wire

1 Attach a shorter length of nylon-coated wire to each of the outside loops of one of the necklace/bracelet ends using a goldfill crimp bead for each but no gimp, following the instructions for Simple Necklace Stringing, page 16. Use a pair of cutting pliers to trim the excess wire.

2 Using the same techniques, attach the two longer lengths of nylon-coated wire to the middle loop, using only one crimp for both wires (diagram A).

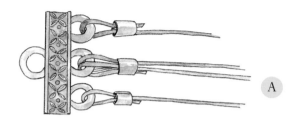

3 Thread onto each of the middle wires three rocailles, one 4mm bead, three rocailles and one beaded rondel.

4 Thread both wires through one large oval bead and another beaded rondel from opposite directions (diagram B).

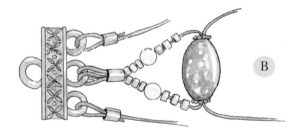

5 Thread onto each of the middle wires three rocailles, one 4mm bead, three rocailles and a beaded rondel. Then thread both wires through another large oval bead and a beaded rondel from opposite ends.

6 Repeat the above step until all the large beads are used or the bracelet is of the required length, finishing with the bead sequence in Step 3, but leaving out the final beaded rondel.

7 Thread both middle wires through a goldfill crimp and then through the middle loop of the other necklace/bracelet end, but DO NOT fix in place, as you will need slack wire to work with. Instead, apply an inexpensive crimp bead at the end of the wires as a temporary 'stopper'.

8 Thread onto one of the two unthreaded wires four rocailles and then thread the wire through the two rocailles on the previously threaded wire that are immediately in front of the beaded rondel. Thread on one rocaille and then thread through the previously threaded two rocailles, 4mm bead and next rocaille.

9 Now thread on one rocaille and then thread through the rocaille immediately in front of the 4mm bead, the 4mm bead itself and the rocaille on the other side (diagram C). Repeat until you reach the end of the bracelet, but finish with the threading sequence in Step 8 in reverse order.

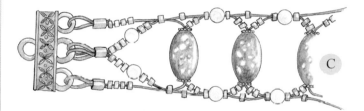

10 Thread on a goldfill crimp bead, but DO NOT fix in place, then thread through the corresponding loop of the necklace/bracelet end and apply an inexpensive crimp bead to the wire as a temporary 'stopper'.

11 Repeat Steps 8–10 with the remaining unthreaded wire, but there is no need to apply a temporary 'stopper' crimp bead.

12 Remove the temporary crimp beads and thread the wires back through the goldfill crimps. After adjusting all the beaded wires to make sure that the beads sit evenly and all loose wire is pulled tight, finish the bracelet by squeezing the crimps onto the wire to secure them firmly in place, as in Step 1.

13 Use a jump ring to attach either part of the clasp to a necklace/bracelet end, following Steps 4–5 of Making a Thong Necklace, page 18.

Roaring Twenties

Ease of making: 5
Time to make: 2 hours
Length: 640mm (25in)

The feature beads in this necklace are from the Italian Pugliani workshop and, with a swirling pattern of mauve roses at their core, they are a tribute to the bead-makers' skills. They were made at least 50 years ago and again are from a stock of old but unused beads. Similar beads are still made, so you should have no difficulty in replicating this necklace with new beads. However, the supplier may still have some of these particular beads left (see Jewelex, page 126).

Once again I have used new beads to complement the larger ones, and I have chosen a design and clasp to match the elegance and quality of these fine old beads.

INGREDIENTS
◎ 10 clear glass-over-rose beads, 12mm
◎ 30 mauve beads, 4mm
◎ small turquoise rocailles
◎ small 'silver'-lined rocailles
◎ 18 silver-plated bead caps, 8mm
◎ 1 silver-plated cone-shaped bead cap, 8mm
◎ 1 silver-plated bead cap, 4mm
◎ 2 'silver' calottes
◎ 1 silver-plated clasp with 'moonstone' cabochon
◎ 3 x 800mm (31½in) lengths of fine monofilament nylon beading thread

1 Tie the three lengths of nylon thread together near to one end in an overhand knot (diagram A).

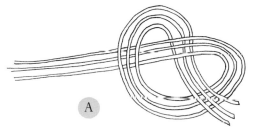

A

2 Trim the excess nylon close to the knot and then briefly touch the cut ends with the flame from a lighted match, but be careful both for your own safety and not to burn away the knot.

3 Thread the free ends of the three strands through the hole of a calotte so that the knot sits inside the 'shell' of the calotte (diagram B).

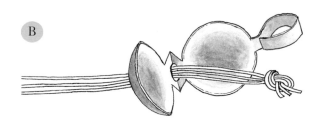

B

9 Thread back up through the 4mm bead cap, the large glass bead and the cone-shaped bead cap. Then, in reverse order, thread on the rocaille sequence only in Step 8.

10 Now thread back up through the central large glass bead and repeat Steps 5–6 four more times to complete the threading (diagram D).

4 Use flat-nosed or general-purpose pliers to squeeze the calotte closed to conceal the knot (diagram C).

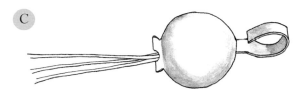

C

5 Thread beads onto one thread in the following sequence: 12 'silver'-lined rocailles, one turquoise rocaille, one 'silver'-lined rocaille, one mauve bead, one 'silver'-lined rocaille, one turquoise rocaille, 12 'silver'-lined rocailles, one 8mm bead cap, one large glass bead and another 8mm bead cap.

6 Repeat the threading sequence eight times and then finish with the rocaille sequence only. Thread through another calotte, but DO NOT close this. Instead, tie a rocaille onto the end of the thread as a temporary 'stopper'.

7 Repeat Steps 5–6 with the second thread, but slightly stagger the position of the mauve beads by replacing the two sets of 12 rocailles with one lot of 10 and another of 14, and take the thread through the bead caps and glass beads.

8 Repeat Steps 5–6 five times with the third thread, but as in Step 7, stagger the position of the mauve beads, this time replacing the sets of 12 rocailles with a 14 and 10. Then, after threading through the central large glass bead of the necklace, thread on beads in the following sequence: seven 'silver'-lined rocailles, one turquoise rocaille, three 'silver'-lined rocailles, the cone-shaped bead cap, a large glass bead, the 4mm bead cap and one more 'silver'-lined rocaille.

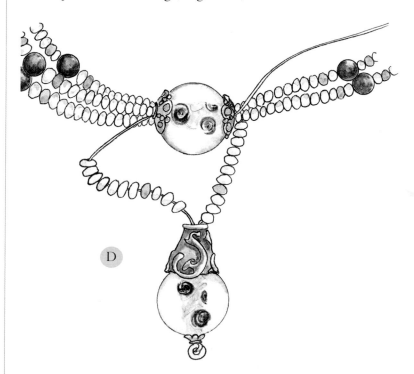

D

11 Remove the temporary 'stopper' beads and adjust the threads so that the beads take up all the slack but leave enough movement for the necklace to drape well, and then follow Steps 1–4 to fix the second calotte over the other knot.

12 Use flat-nosed or general-purpose pliers to attach the clasp to the necklace by opening the loops of the calotte sideways and then closing them.

MURANO MIRACLES

Venice is considered by many to be the 'home' of quality ornamental glass. The original purpose of glass beads was to imitate precious gems and thus they were initially formed in simple plain colours. Later, they were made in huge quantities to supply the demand for rosary beads, but as trade developed, skilled bead makers experimented with new designs and eventually produced highly decorative beads with a correspondingly high market value. In 1292, because of extreme fire risks from the furnaces and the need to keep the unique bead-making techniques secret, the glass- and bead-making factories were moved to the island of Murano.

The beads of Venice played a large part in trade between Europe and Africa, and vast shiploads of beads were traded for African furs, ivory, gold and, unfortunately, slaves. Beads became an extremely valuable 'currency', so much so that in Ghana the name for a bead, 'cedi', subsequently became the name of the country's monetary unit. The strings of beads seen here (old trade beads) have subsequently been imported from Ghana and are now so sought after that they are a valuable export item.

Today's Venetian glass beads are still among the foremost for both design and quality, and I have chosen some stunning examples for the jewellery in this section.

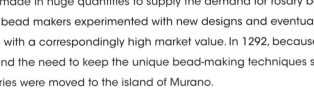

Venetian Dream Necklace

└ Ease of making: 3
└ Time to make: 90 minutes
└ Length: 380mm (15in)

This gorgeous choker is made from a combination of beautiful glass lamp beads and vibrant rocailles in matching colours. The beads are strung on nylon-coated wire, which has enough spring to give form to the circular shapes and also makes the necklace very comfortable to wear because the curve of the wire provides flexibility. Although the necklace looks complicated, it is quite simple to make and simply involves the threading of two lengths of wire that travel through the main bead in opposite directions.

INGREDIENTS

- ◎ 11 blue/green baroque lamp beads, 12mm
- ◎ large (5mm) green-lined rocailles
- ◎ small white pearl rocailles
- ◎ medium blue rocailles
- ◎ 52 silver-plated bead caps, 4mm
- ◎ 22 silver-plated beaded rondels, 4mm
- ◎ 4 silver-plated jump rings
- ◎ 2 sterling silver crimp beads
- ◎ 1 silver-plated 'S' clasp
- ◎ 2 x 800mm (31½in) lengths of nylon-coated wire

1 Follow the instructions for Simple Necklace Stringing, page 16, to thread both lengths of wire through a crimp bead, thread on two jump rings and then, forming a loop that holds the two jump rings, thread both wires back through the crimp bead. Squeeze the crimp bead onto the wires and trim the excess wire close to the crimp.

2 Thread onto both wires together two blue rocailles, one white pearl rocaille, one bead cap, one large green-lined rocaille, one bead cap and one white pearl rocaille.

3 The wires now divide, and onto one wire thread five blue rocailles, one white pearl rocaille, one bead cap, one large green-lined rocaille, one bead cap, five blue rocailles and a beaded rondel.

4 Thread the other wire following the sequence in Step 3, but instead of five blue rocailles thread six in each instance. This has the effect of curving the necklace slightly so that it sits well against the neck (diagram A).

6 Repeat Steps 3–5 ten more times or until the necklace is of the required length, but make sure that the lower edge of the necklace has all the sequences of six blue rocailles and the top has the fives, otherwise the curve of the necklace will be lost.

7 Complete the necklace by following Steps 1–4 in reverse order.

8 The clasp for this necklace is a simple hook at either end. Attach to one pair of jump rings and use your pliers to gently close the hook so that it will not become accidentally detached.

5 Now thread both wires through the large lamp bead from opposite directions (diagram A).

Summer Days

— Ease of making: 3
— Time to make: 45 minutes
└ Length: 75mm (3in)

Summer sunshine and garden flowers are brought to mind by the colours of this pretty pair of earrings, and the toning hue of the anodized niobium ear-wires and headpins enhances the delicate effect. The main featured beads are again old but unused, from the US supplier Jewelex (see page 126), originating from the renowned Farkalarta family in Murano. To match their fine quality, I have teamed them with Swarovski crystal.

These earrings look difficult to make, but in fact are just as easy as the simplest pair. However, there are ten loops to make, so they will take longer and will thoroughly test your loop-forming abilities. Look carefully at the photograph for the threading sequence and then follow the steps for making up the basic earrings, remembering to tape your pliers to avoid damaging the anodized colour of the niobium headpins and ear-hooks.

INGREDIENTS
⊙ 2 'gold'-foiled baroque Venetian beads, 12mm
⊙ 2 clear Swarovski crystal beaded rondels, 3mm
⊙ 4 rose-coloured Swarovski crystal bicone beads, 4mm
⊙ 2 AB-coated Swarovski faceted round beads, 4mm
⊙ 6 AB-coated Swarovski bicone beads, 3mm
⊙ 10 goldfill oval beads, 2 x 4mm
⊙ 4 gold-plated beaded rondels, 4mm
⊙ 2 gold-plated faceted bicone beads, 3mm
⊙ 2 fuschia anodized niobium headpins, 50mm
⊙ 4 green anodized niobium headpins, 50mm
⊙ 2 fuschia anodized niobium straight-leg angular ear-hooks

1 Cut the head off one of the green niobium headpins and then make a loop in one end, following Steps 3 and 5 of Basic Earring Making, page 18. Thread on the main bead, a Swarovski clear crystal beaded rondel and a goldfill oval bead. Trim the excess headpin wire, if necessary, and make another loop in the headpin.

2 Thread your beads onto the other green headpin and one of the fuschia headpins, referring to the photograph. Make a loop at the top end of the fuschia headpin and attach it to the loop beneath the large bead. Trim a short piece from the end of the green headpin so that it will hang slightly above the first drop, then form a loop and attach to the loop beneath the large bead.

3 Repeat Steps 1–2 for the other earring. Make up the ear-hooks referring to the photograph and following the instructions for Tailor-making Ear-hooks, page 19, then attach to the beaded drops to complete.

Golden Swirls

├─Ease of making: 4
├─Time to make: 15 minutes
└─Length: 55mm (2in)

I have chosen more beautiful 'gold'-foiled Fakalarta beads for this relatively simple pair of earrings and I have jointed them in the middle of the drop to give movement to the finished pieces. The ear-wires are made from goldfill and are therefore unlikely to cause allergy problems.

INGREDIENTS

◎ 2 'gold'-foiled baroque Venetian glass beads, 14mm
◎ 4 gold-plated beaded rondels, 4mm
◎ 2 faceted round blue Czech glass beads, 4mm
◎ 4 goldfill oval beads, 2 x 4mm
◎ 4 gold-plated bead caps, 4mm
◎ 2 blue anodized niobium coils
◎ 4 goldfill headpins, 50mm
◎ 2 goldfill straight-leg ear-hooks

If you have made the previous pair of earrings, then these are easy! Just refer to the photograph for the threading sequence and follow the instructions for Basic Earring Making, page 18. The only variation in the design is that the central section of beads is threaded onto a separate beaded headpin, with loops at either end.

GLASS WITH CLASS

I t is not only Venice that produces high-quality glass beads. Some of our finest beads come from the area of Europe collectively known as Bohemia, where the bead-making tradition goes back many centuries. In the 1500s there were dozens of bead-making glassworks in operation in the Bavarian/Bohemian forests. Today, there are fewer manufacturers, but the choice of beads available to us from this region is immense and beautiful beads are produced in great numbers with a quality to compete with their Italian rivals. However, despite this, most Bohemian beads are usually less expensive than their renowned cousins.

Indian glass beads are also plentiful, inexpensive and the range of colour and design is huge. Also, most are handmade lamp beads that are produced in the home of the maker – see page 9 for a brief account of their method of production.

Coming Up Roses

- Ease of making: 3
- Time to make: 1 hour
- Length: 400mm (15¾in)

Here, a garland of Bohemian glass roses, simply and haphazardly strung, creates a dainty summer necklace. Strictly speaking, the roses that I have used are not beads, as there is no hole directly through the glass. Instead, during manufacture, a looped wire is fused into the centre of the back and this is used for threading. I have chosen two different types of flower, with the majority being open single roses in a matt finish, and the others a double rose in a glossy finish. The 'silver'-foiled cone-shaped beads at either end are also Bohemian and are chosen as a lead-in to the twisted wire strands that complete the necklace. In keeping with the floral theme, I have chosen an unusual sterling silver trailing leaf clasp, which has a simple hook-and-eye closure for easy fastening

INGREDIENTS

- ◎ 50 frosted glass single roses
- ◎ 10 glossy glass double mauve roses
- ◎ 10 glossy glass double pink roses
- ◎ 2 'silver'-foiled glass cone-shaped beads, 18 x 8mm
- ◎ 2 jump rings, 5mm
- ◎ 4 square calotte crimps
- ◎ 2 x 8mm (³⁄₈in) lengths of mauve gimp
- ◎ 1 sterling silver hook-and-eye clasp
- ◎ 250mm (10in) length of nylon-coated wire
- ◎ 800mm (31½in) length of pink jewellery wire
- ◎ 800mm (31½in) length of mauve jewellery wire
- ◎ 800mm (31½in) length of 'silver' jewellery wire

1 Place one end of all three lengths of jewellery wire together and use general-purpose pliers to form a small loop in the wires, then twist the wires together until the loop is secure. Repeat with the other end of the wires (diagram A).

2 Hook one loop over a picture hook or something similar and then insert a pencil through the loop at the other end and twist it until all the wires are twisted together (see Steps 2–3 of Flora, page 67). Be careful to pull downwards while twisting, otherwise the wire will flip off the picture hook.

3 When the wires are satisfactorily twisted, remove from the hook, fold the wire in half and repeat the twisting process to form a thicker wire rope.

4 When you are satisfied that the wires have formed a reasonably thick and attractive wire rope, use cutting pliers to cut it into two sections of the required length – in this case, 100mm (4in). Use flat-nosed or general-purpose pliers to firmly apply a square calotte crimp to each end of the wire rope sections, following Steps 2–3 of Making a Thong Necklace, page 18.

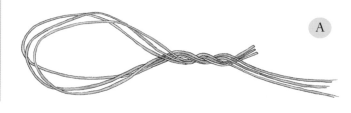

A

5 Attach one end of the nylon-coated wire to the square calotte crimp at the end of one section of wire rope using one length of gimp, following the instructions for Simple Necklace Stringing, page 16.

6 Thread one of the cone-shaped beads onto the nylon-coated wire, followed by all the glass flowers, making sure that they are threaded in random sequence,

but with the coloured roses spread fairly evenly among the frosted ones. Finish by threading on the other cone-shaped bead and attaching the beaded wire to the square calotte crimp at one end of the second section of wire rope, as in Step 5.

7 Use jump rings to attach the clasp to the calotte crimps at the other ends of the wire rope, following Steps 4–5 of Making a Thong Necklace, page 18.

Bohemian Drops

- Ease of making: 3
- Time to make: 15 minutes
- Length: 60mm (2½in)

To show another application for the cone-shaped beads featured in the previous necklace, I have used a different colourway here to make a pair of drop earrings. Alternatively, you could use the same colour as those in the necklace to make a matching set. I just love these beads, which incorporate delicate swathes of pink, blue and green glass over a 'silver'-foiled core, covered beneath a perfect surface layer of clear glass. The ear-hooks are sterling silver and, as is my preference, are supplied unmade. The main beads are all sterling silver or silver-plated pewter.

INGREDIENTS

- 2 'silver'-foiled glass cone-shaped beads, 8 x 8mm
- 2 silver-plated beads, 8mm
- 2 beaded rondels, 6 x 3mm
- 2 silver-plated washer beads, 4mm
- 4 sterling silver oval beads, 4 x 2mm
- 2 'silver'-lined mauve rocailles
- 2 sterling silver headpins, 50mm
- 2 sterling silver straight-leg ear-hooks

To make up the earrings, refer to the photograph for the threading sequence and follow the instructions for Basic Earring Making, page 18.

Indian Ocean Blues

- Ease of making: 4
- Time to make: 1½ hours
- Length: 580mm (23in)

The beads in this necklace have a lustrous sheen that conjures up a vision of the calm, glistening blue seas of the Indian Ocean. It would look equally good as an item to dress up a wedding outfit or to wear with jeans and a summer top. The beads are inexpensive, but well made with, usefully for this particular design, a large hole that makes them both easy to thread and allows for the passage of several threads. The project is not the simplest, but even a beginner should be able to complete it.

INGREDIENTS

- ◎ 9 lustred glass ovals, 20 x 12mm
- ◎ 26 lustred glass discs, 7mm
- ◎ 60 lustred round glass beads, 6mm
- ◎ 12 medium rocailles in a matching colour
- ◎ 10 'silver' cone-shaped bead caps
- ◎ 2 'silver' faceted bicone beads, 5mm
- ◎ 4 'silver' crimp beads
- ◎ 2 x 8mm (³⁄₈in) lengths of 'silver' gimp
- ◎ 1 'silver' toggle clasp
- ◎ 610mm (24in) length of nylon-coated wire
- ◎ 2 x 400mm (15¾in) lengths of nylon-coated wire

1 Attach one end of the single length of nylon-coated wire to the toggle clasp using one crimp bead and one length of gimp, following the instructions for Simple Necklace Stringing, page 16. Thread 11 x 7mm glass discs onto the wire.

2 Thread a crimp bead onto the same wire. Pass the ends of the two shorter lengths of wire through this crimp bead. Making sure that the ends are hidden beneath one or two glass discs and that all these beads are pushed up to the clasp, use general-purpose pliers to squeeze the crimp onto the wire (diagram A).

A

3 Thread a cone-shaped bead cap over all three wires, followed by three large glass oval beads, another bead cap, a 7mm glass disc and one more bead cap. Now onto each of the three wires thread one rocaille, followed by ten 6mm round beads and one more rocaille. Then thread a bead cap and a glass disc onto all three wires together.

4 Repeat Step 3 once, but between the oval beads thread on a faceted bicone bead. After threading on the glass disc onto all three wires, thread on a bead cap and three oval beads, followed by another bead cap.

5 You now have two short and one long wire emerging from the last bead cap. Thread a crimp bead onto all three wires together, and after ensuring that the beads of the necklace all sit correctly on the wires and no wire is left visible, use your pliers to squeeze the crimp bead onto the wires to secure.

6 Use cutting pliers to trim the excess wire from the two shorter lengths, leaving 10mm (½in) spare. Thread on 11 disc beads, making sure that the spare wire is hidden inside the first one or two, and complete the necklace by attaching to the clasp, as in Step 1.

CZECH IT OUT

Many of the beads that come from the prolific bead-producing Czech Republic are known as Bohemian, and some of these were featured in the previous section – see pages 30–32. Those used in this section are also Czech, but are of a different type, with the vast majority being pressed, or mass produced. They vary from faceted glass to imitation pearls and are of such fine quality that the seam that often betrays the origins of pressed beads is very difficult, if not impossible, to see. I find these beads indispensable and throughout the book you will find many examples of these Czech products in a wide range of colours, sizes and shapes.

Autumn Hues

- Ease of making: 4
- Time to make: 3 hours
- Length: 540mm (21¼in)

This necklace is made up of over 20 different examples of the huge and varied range of Czech beads. I have chosen autumnal hues and mixed them with a variety of gold beads, and then used rat-tail in graduated shades of brown to complete the mellow look. This necklace is made in a princess length, but it looks equally good as a choker. At first glance it might appear difficult or complicated to make, but in fact the main skill required is patience!

INGREDIENTS

- 250–300 beads in a mix of autumn shades and 'gold', ranging in size from 4mm rounds to 18 x 10mm ovals
- 2 beads for use as temporary 'stoppers'
- 6 'gold' jump rings, 4mm
- 6 'gold' square calotte crimps
- 1 gold-plated necklace clasp to take 3 strands
- 1½–2m (60–80in) 'gold' jewellery wire
- 2 x 510mm (20in) lengths of shaded rat-tail
- 560mm (22in) length of shaded rat-tail

1 Tie a bead onto one end of the jewellery wire to act as a temporary 'stopper' to prevent the threaded beads from falling off.

2 Thread all the beads onto the wire in a completely random sequence, but be careful not to include any large beads within the first and last 20. Leave about 150mm (6in) of wire spare at either end and tie on another temporary 'stopper' bead to the other end of

the wire, then set this aside while you make up the remainder of the necklace.

3 Attach the two 510mm (20in) lengths of rat-tail to the two outside loops of one part of the clasp using square calotte crimps and jump rings, following the instructions for Making a Thong Necklace, page 18. Then attach the longer length of rat-tail to the centre loop of the clasp in the same way.

4 Tie the longer length of rat-tail in an overhand knot around the other two lengths 160mm (6¼in) from the calotte crimps (diagram A).

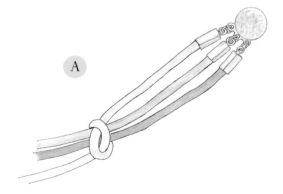

A

5 Use the same length of rat-tail to tie another overhand knot over the other two lengths 180mm (7in) from the original knot. Now trim all the rat-tail strands to the same length, i.e. 160mm (6¼in) from the last knot. Attach the other part of the clasp to the three strands of rat-tail, as in Step 3.

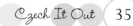

6 Remove the 'stopper' bead from the beaded length of wire, then cut the wire end to ensure that it is quite straight. Thread the end through one of the knots in the rat-tail strands, threading towards the clasp (diagram B).

7 Now usc about 100mm (4in) of the wire to wind as neatly as possible around the three threads to secure in place. Finish by folding the end of the wire over so that it cannot stick into the wearer of the necklace, then tuck it out of sight beneath the knot (diagram C).

8 Using a pencil for additional support, wind the beaded wire around the rat-tail (and pencil) to form a spiral, then remove the pencil and follow Steps 6–7 to finish the necklace by securely fastening the beads in place.

Golden Rain Brooch

— Ease of making: 3
— Time to make: 30 minutes
— Length: 60mm (2½in) plus 40mm (1½in) drop

The large oval bead in this project also appears in the previous necklace, but to show an alternative use, I have teamed it here with smaller teardrop beads to form the focus of an unusual brooch. The base on which the beads are threaded is actually a hatpin, appropriately bent to form a simple brooch bar.

INGREDIENTS
◎ 1 lustred glass oval bead, 19 x 8mm
◎ 3 lustred glass teardrop beads, 9 x 6mm
◎ 4 gold-plated fancy metal cube beads, 7 x 6mm
◎ 2 gold-plated beaded rondels, 6 x 4mm
◎ 6 gold-plated bead caps, 3mm
◎ 2 matt 'gold' beads, 2.5mm
◎ medium amber AB-coated rocailles
◎ 1 'gold' hatpin, 150mm
◎ 3 'gold' headpins, 50mm
◎ 2 goldfill crimp beads
◎ 2 x 8mm (³/₈in) lengths of 'gold' gimp
◎ 100mm (4in) length of nylon-coated wire

1 Use flat-nosed pliers to bend the hatpin at a right angle 5mm (¼in) from the 'head' end, to form the 'keeper' to the brooch (diagram A).

2 Form another right-angle bend in the same direction 5mm (¼ in) from the first one (diagram B).

3 Make a third right-angle bend in a direction towards the main length of wire 5mm (¼in) from the previous right-angle bend (diagram C).

4 Bend the 'head' of the pin in slightly towards the wire to narrow the gap (diagram D).

D ──

5 Refer to the photograph opposite for the threading sequence and use the headpins to form three small drops, following the instructions for Basic Earring Making, page 18.

6 Make up the central looped drop by forming a loop in the nylon-coated wire using a goldfill crimp bead and a length of gimp, following the instructions for Simple Necklace Stringing, page 16, then threading on 12 rocailles, one of the beaded drops and another 12

rocailles. Form a loop at the other end of the wire as at the beginning.

7 Thread all the beads and drops onto the hatpin in the sequence shown in the photograph. Then, because of variations in bead size, check with a ruler that there is enough spare wire remaining so that when it is bent towards the clasp there is enough length for the pointed end to reach and fit into the 'keeper'.

8 Immediately next to the last bead, use flat-nosed or general-purpose pliers to bend the hatpin at a right angle towards the 'keeper'. Finally, make a right-angle bend 5mm (¼in) from the previous one, again towards the 'keeper' so that the point just fits inside to form the catch of the brooch.

Rose Pink

- Ease of making: 3
- Time to make: 5 hours
- Length: 470mm (18½in) plus 50mm (2in) pendant

This necklace showcases the many delightful shades of colour in the Czech range of beads, incorporating six different pinks and mauves. However, you could choose to make the same necklace in another colour and find just as many subtle shades of blue, green, red or brown. The beads, which are made in various sizes of round, oval and teardrop shapes, are precision-formed pressed glass and very useful in jewellery where uniformity is required. The pendant is a beautiful enamelled Chinese bead, which is also available in other colours and designs.

I do not often use monofilament nylon, but in this necklace it is very useful because it is flexible and fine enough to allow four threads through the hole of one bead. The interlinking clasp is the same at each end and provides attachment loops for three calottes each. Once more the greatest skill needed to complete the project is patience; if you tackle this one, you will be threading just under 1,500 beads!

INGREDIENTS

◎ 6 x 250 AB-coated faceted beads in various shades of
  pink to light mauve, 4mm
◎ 1 enamelled disc bead, 42mm
◎ 1 bead for use as a temporary 'stopper'
◎ 1 'silver' headpin, 75mm
◎ 6 silver-plated calottes
◎ 2 'gold' square calotte crimps
◎ 1 silver-plated interlinking clasp to take 3 strands
◎ 2 x 50mm (2in) lengths of suede in colours to suit
  the beads
◎ 12 x 600mm (24in) lengths of monofilament nylon
  beading thread
◎ flexible twisted wire beading needle (optional)

1 Place one end of four lengths of nylon thread close
together and tie in a simple tight overhand knot
(diagram A).

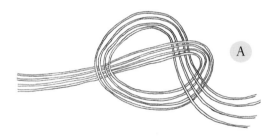

2 Use sharp scissors to neaten the short ends of the
knot so that the knot and the ends will fit inside one
of the silver-plated calottes, then briefly touch the cut
ends with the flame from a lighted match, but be careful
both for your own safety and not to burn away the knot.
Thread the free ends through the hole of a calotte so
that the knot sits inside the 'shell' of the calotte
(diagram B).

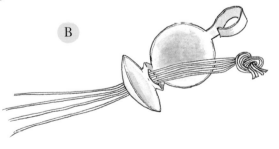

3 Use flat-nosed or general-purpose pliers to squeeze
the calotte closed to conceal the knot, then attach
the calotte to a loop of the clasp (diagram C).

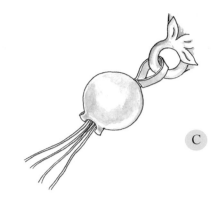

4 Place each shade of the 250 x 4mm beads in a
separate shallow container on your tray. Choosing
one colour, thread 125 of these beads onto one of the
four threads. You may find it easier to use a beading
needle for this task, although with monofilament nylon
thread this is not essential.

5 When you have threaded all the beads, leave 100mm
(4in) of thread spare so that the beads are loose, and
near the end of the thread, tie on a 'stopper' bead of any
type to secure your threaded beads on the monofilament
nylon thread.

6 Thread all three of the remaining threads through
the first two beads next to the calotte (diagram D,
middle strand).

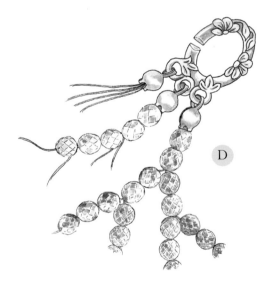

7 Thread one of the three threads through the next
two of the previously threaded beads (diagram D,
middle strand). Now thread 117 beads of another shade
onto this thread.

8 When you have threaded on all the beads, pass this thread through the last four beads of the original beaded thread and, again leaving 100m (4in) of spare thread, tie the thread onto the 'stopper' bead.

9 Thread one of the remaining two unbeaded threads with 121 beads of another shade. When you have threaded on all the beads, pass this thread through the last two beads of the previously threaded beads and, as before, tie the thread to the 'stopper' bead.

10 Thread the last remaining thread with 117 beads of another shade, then pass this thread through the last two beads of those threaded in Step 9 and, like the previous three threads, through the last two previously threaded beads.

11 The threaded beads next to the calotte should now appear as the fully beaded section of diagram D, while at the other end of the necklace the beads remain loose but attached to the 'stopper' bead. Untie and remove the 'stopper' bead. Leaving a little movement of beads on the thread, to allow for twisting of the necklace, make sure that most of the slack is taken up and then follow Steps 1–3 to attach a calotte and fasten it to the clasp.

12 Repeat all the instructions above twice more to complete the threading and attach the beaded threads to the remaining loops of the clasp. Each shade of bead should be used twice.

13 Use general-purpose pliers to bend the looped end of a square calotte crimp in towards the middle and squeeze it so that it will not be seen when the crimp is closed (diagram E).

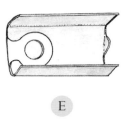

E

14 Form a loop in one length of suede, meeting end to end, and place centrally in the calotte crimp. Use flat-nosed or general-purpose pliers to carefully close the 'wings' of the calotte crimp over the suede, making sure that they don't slip, to hold it in place (diagram F). Repeat with the other calotte crimp and length of suede.

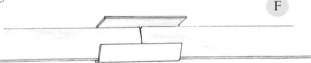

F

15 Thread one of the leftover beads onto the headpin, then the large enamelled pendant bead. Form a loop in the headpin, following Steps 3–5 of Basic Earring Making, page 18, but before closing the loop, thread on the loops of suede. Close the wire loop, making sure it is tight so that your finished pendant does not spin on the headpin.

16 Thread your suede-looped pendant over the threaded beads and your necklace is finished. You can wear the beaded threads twisted, as shown, or, for a looser look, untwisted.

Black Magic

─ Ease of making: 6
─ Time to make: 5 hours
─ Length: 360mm (14¼in) plus 130mm (5in) drops

This is perfect for the party season and other dressy occasions. All the beads in this necklace are Czech and they shine just like the best-quality jet, a natural stone formed by fossilized coal popular in Victorian times. The necklace would look equally good made with alternative beads, for example pearls or crystal.

This is not a simple 'string-in-an-hour' necklace, and will take at least half a day and a lot of patience to complete. However, the result is worth it, and you will feel million-dollar glamorous when you wear it!

The main body of the necklace is strung on nylon-coated wire, which lends it a springy, stretchy quality that is particularly useful in a choker. The drops are on beading thread to give a fluidity of movement. To demonstrate a new technique, I have used an alternative method of attaching the necklace to the clasp.

INGREDIENTS

- 453 black faceted beads, 3mm
- 203 black faceted beads, 4mm
- 4 black faceted beads, 6mm
- 9 black faceted teardrop beads, 7 x 5mm
- 12 black faceted teardrop beads, 9 x 7mm
- 5 black faceted teardrop beads, 13 x 9mm
- 2 black metal calottes
- 25 black metal crimp beads
- 1 black faceted acrylic cabochon
- 1 'gold' clasp for setting the cabochon, 14 x 10mm
- 2 x 700mm (27½in) lengths of black fine nylon-coated wire
- 2.5m (100in) length of black beading thread
- epoxy glue
- bottle of liquid superglue or a flexible twisted wire beading needle

1 Following the glue manufacturer's instructions, use the epoxy glue to stick the cabochon in the clasp setting and set aside for the glue to harden.

2 Thread one of the crimp beads onto the ends of the two lengths of nylon-coated wire and use flat-nosed or general-purpose pliers to squeeze it onto the wire. Trim any excess wire close to the crimp.

3 Thread the free ends of the wires through the hole in the calotte and pull them down until the crimp bead is inside the 'shell' of the calotte. Use the pliers to squeeze the calotte closed to conceal the crimp bead and the ends of the wire (diagram A).

4 Thread one 3mm faceted bead onto both wires, then thread separately onto each wire four 3mm faceted beads. Thread onto one of the wires one more 3mm faceted bead, then thread the other wire back through this bead in the opposite direction, to form a loop – see Step 5/diagram A of Venetian Dream Necklace, page 28.

5 Thread five 3mm faceted beads onto each wire. Thread onto one of the wires one more 3mm faceted bead, then thread the other wire back through this bead in the opposite direction, to form another beaded loop.

6 Repeat Step 5 seventeen more times or until the necklace is of the required length. Finish the base of the necklace by repeating Steps 2–4 in reverse order.

7 Now prepare the thread for threading the central drop of your necklace. Use scissors to diagonally cut a 360mm (14in) length of beading thread, then dip the first 50mm (2in) of the thread briefly into the bottle of superglue, to stiffen it. Have a tissue at hand to wipe off the excess glue and take care not to spill any onto yourself or your beads. Alternatively, use a flexible twisted wire beading needle if you prefer.

8 Tie an overhand knot in the other end of the thread, then thread on one black metal crimp bead and slide it

B

down onto the knot, making sure that both ends of thread are inside the crimp (diagram B). Use pliers to gently squeeze the crimp over the thread close to the knot; make sure it is secure without cutting through the thread.

9 Thread on one of the 13 x 9mm faceted teardrop beads, followed by two 6mm faceted beads, one 7 x 5mm faceted teardrop bead, 11 x 4mm faceted beads and 15 x 3mm faceted beads.

10 Attach the drop to the necklace base by threading through the middle bead of one side of the central circle. Continue with the same thread to make the next drop of beads and thread on beads in the following sequence: 15 x 3mm faceted beads, 11 x 4mm faceted beads, one 7 x 5mm teardrop bead, one 6mm faceted bead and finally one 13 x 9mm teardrop bead. Follow Step 8 to secure in place, threading back up through the first teardrop bead to hide the end of the thread. Use scissors to cut off the excess thread. Note that this drop is shorter in length than the first drop, as part of the graduated style of the design.

11 Repeat Steps 7–10, following the threading sequences in diagram C to make the remaining drops, but remember to decrease the length of thread used as the drops get shorter.

12 As you can see, the drops are made in pairs, with one always being slightly longer than its partner. Therefore, to make an even number of drops on either side of the central drop, the last drop on one side needs to be threaded as a single drop. To do this, thread the required beads onto the thread, then loop the thread over the wire of the appropriate loop and thread back down through the beads. Tie a knot in both threads close to the last bead and as before slide a crimp onto the knot and squeeze to secure.

13 Use general-purpose pliers to open the loop of each calotte sideways and attach to the clasp.

Numbers given beside the drops indicate the number of 3mm and 4mm faceted beads to use

3mm

4mm

CRYSTAL GAZING

There are two types of crystal bead. The most readily available is crystal glass and comes in a wide variety of both brilliant and subtle colours. The accepted master in the manufacture of these sparkling faceted beads is the Austrian company, Swarovski, but there are other up-and-coming imitators in other countries, such as China.

The other type, which rarely has the sparkle of a cut glass crystal bead, is made from one of our most commonly occurring natural stones, rock crystal or quartz. Rock crystal is an alternative birthstone to the diamond for April, or the zodiac sign Aries, and the two stones are believed to share many of the same mystical qualities. Rock crystal is reputed to bring courage, ensure peaceful sleep and protect against evil. Many centuries ago, prior to our knowledge of how to release a diamond's fire by creating facets, quartz was the more prized of the two stones because, in its raw state, it was more appealing to the eye. One of the most familiar types of quartz is the clear rock crystal form, but coloured varieties are also available, such as smoky or rose quartz, amethyst or citrine.

The two types of crystal bead lend themselves to different types of jewellery, the cut glass variety being ideal for party wear, while the natural material is more suitable for everyday wear.

Icicle Choker

- Ease of making: 4
- Time to make: 1½ hours
- Length: 400mm (15¾in) plus 60mm (2½in) drops

This project has a strong contemporary appeal. As its main feature I have chosen a large quartz point crystal. The shape of the stone is natural, with just the addition of a hole, but the colour is not. To achieve this attractive crackled colour effect, the quartz has been infused with dye. The accompanying beads are a mixture of many different types, from Czech cut glass to freshwater pearl.

Other colours and sizes of quartz point are available, such as pink, purple and green, so you could change the look of your necklace by using one of these alternatives, together with a different choice of supplementary beads. An alternative design using three of these quartz points simply separated by 'gold' large-holed beads is shown top-left on the opposite page. These are 'strung' onto a purpose made thick choker wire, which has a simple screw-off ball at one end for easy 'threading'.

1 Bend the anodized niobium wire in two and twist the two lengths together. To make this easier, follow Steps 2–3 of Flora, page 67. However, remember that you only need two pieces of wire twisted together and also that this niobium wire is springier than ordinary expensive jewellery wire and therefore is more difficult to twist.

2 Use cutting or general-purpose pliers to cut one of the ends of the twisted wires to an even length. Apply one part of the clasp by pushing it over the cut ends and then, fairly gently, use flat-nosed or general-purpose pliers to squeeze the silver tube end of the clasp down onto the wires. Check that the clasp is held securely on the wires.

3 Refer to the photograph to thread up the drops, following the instructions for Basic Earring Making, page 18. Cut the chain to varying lengths and attach to the headpins. Attach jump rings to the other ends of the chain for threading onto the wire.

INGREDIENTS

- 1 quartz point crystal, 40 x 18mm
- 1 Czech crystal teardrop bead, 12 x 10mm
- 1 Czech crystal teardrop bead, 10 x 7mm
- 1 oval blue lace agate bead, 17 x 13mm
- 1 lapis lazuli bead, 10mm
- 1 peacock blue square freshwater pearl, 10 x 10mm
- 1 'silver'-lined blue baroque-style glass bead, 15 x 10mm
- 1 blue crackle glass bead, 6mm
- 1 imitation opal bead, 6mm
- 10 'silver' beaded rondels, 7mm
- 4 silver-plated plain washer beads, 4mm
- 7 'silver' beads, 2mm
- 2 fancy 'silver' beads, 4mm
- 8 'silver' headpins 50mm
- 8 'silver' jump rings
- 900mm (35in) length of blue anodized niobium wire
- 1 sterling silver crimp clasp
- 120mm (4¾in) length of 'silver' curb chain

4 Thread all the drops onto the wire, with the large crystal set close to the centre, and separate each drop with a beaded rondel.

5 Check your choker for size and trim any spare wire if necessary before repeating Step 2 to apply the other part of the clasp.

Amber Collar

- Ease of making: 8
- Time to make: 4 hours
- Length: 420mm (16½in)
  plus pendant 40mm (1½in) pendant

The crystal elements of this necklace are the amber glass pendant drop and the gorgeous 4mm sparkling crystal bicones. Both are manufactured by the famous Austrian company Swarovski, whose glass products are renowned for their brilliance and perfection. The pendant in particular is so stunning that it deserves a spectacular setting, so I spent many hours designing a necklace from which to suspend it. The finished item is made to fit closely to the neck, like a collar, and to achieve that effect for all sizes of neck I have used a chain-and-hook-type fastening that can be adjusted. The surplus chain has a 'golden' pendant, which hangs gracefully down the back of the neck to complete the elegant evening look.

INGREDIENTS

- 1 amber Swarovski crystal teardrop, 24 x 12mm
- about 258 cube beads, 4mm
- 102 light topaz Swarovski crystal bicone beads, 4mm
- small 'gold'-lined rocailles
- medium 'gold' AB-coated rocailles
- 1 'gold' crackle-effect bead, 8mm
- 41 gold-plated beaded rondels, 6 x 4mm
- 2 gold-plated bead caps, 4mm
- 1 gold-plated cone-shaped bead cap, 8mm
- 3 gold plated 5-hole spacer bars
- 1 'gold' headpin, 50mm
- 1 'gold' triangle jump
- 10 goldfill crimp beads
- 10 inexpensive crimp beads for use as temporary 'stoppers'
- 10 x 8mm (³⁄₈in) lengths of 'gold' gimp
- 2 gold-plated 5–1 necklace ends
- 1 'gold' hook clasp
- 150mm (6in) length of heavyweight 'gold' open-link curb chain
- 5 x 450mm (17¾in) lengths of nylon-coated wire
- 100mm (4in) length of monofilament nylon beading thread

1 Thread one end of each length of wire through a loop in one of the 5–1 necklace ends, but DO NOT secure them at this stage as you may need to make adjustments later. Instead, thread an inexpensive crimp bead onto each wire and use general-purpose pliers to squeeze onto the wire close to the end to act as a temporary 'stopper' (diagram A).

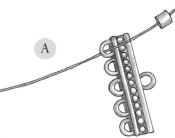

2 Carefully following the threading sequence in the photograph, thread the beads and spacer bars onto one length of wire at a time and finish by threading the ends through the loops of the other necklace end. As in Step 1, apply an inexpensive crimp to the end of each wire as a temporary 'stopper'.

3 Once threaded, check to make sure that the necklace sits well against the neck. If not, add or remove beads from both ends. Also check for mistakes.

4 When you are satisfied with your threading, attach the ends of the wires to the necklace ends, using goldfill crimp beads and gimp, following the instructions for Simple Necklace Stringing, page 16.

5 Refer to the photograph for the threading sequence to make up the drop for the necklace back, using the headpin and following the instructions for Basic Earring Making, page 18. Attach it to one end of the chain by opening a link, opening it sideways, as with a jump ring.

6 Open up the last link of the chain at the other end and remove it, then remove the next link. Attach these two links to the loop on one of the necklace ends. Attach the hook clasp to the end link.

7 Open the last link of the longer length of chain and attach it to the loop on the other necklace end.

8 Use flat-nosed or general-purpose pliers to attach the triangle jump ring to the crystal teardrop (diagram B).

9 Loop the length of nylon thread around the lower necklace strand, in the position as seen in the photograph, and then secure this in place by tying the nylon thread in an overhand knot around itself (diagram C). Thread on ten AB-coated rocailles, a 4mm bead cap, the crystal drop, another 4mm bead cap and ten more AB-coated rocailles. Knot the nylon thread as before. Make sure that both knots are tied tightly and that the looped beads are hanging well, with no spare nylon thread showing, before using a pair of sharp scissors to trim any excess nylon thread.

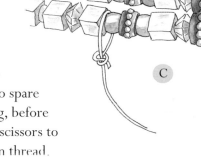

Crystal Chains

Ease of making: 3
Time to make: 75 minutes
Length: 100mm (4in)

These feminine earrings swing with graceful movement and owe their diamond-like brilliance to the various small Swarovski crystal beads that hang from the silver curb chains. They are simple but time consuming to make.

INGREDIENTS

2 Swarovski crystal bicone beads, 4mm
10 Swarovski crystal bicone beads, 3mm
8 Swarovski crystal round beads, 4mm
2 Swarovski crystals, 5 x 7mm
2 sterling silver beads, 2mm
20 fine sterling silver headpins, 50mm
2 x 70mm (2¾in) lengths of sterling silver curb chain
2 sterling silver straight-leg angular ear-hooks

1 Make up the ear-hooks, following the instructions for Tailor-making Ear-hooks, page 19.

2 Thread each bead onto a headpin, then follow Steps 3–5 of Basic Earring Making, page 18, to trim the excess wire of each headpin and form a loop.

3 Attach the headpins to the chains, with the largest oval bead hanging from the bottom link, as shown. Attach the chains to the ear-hooks.

Rainbow Choker

- Ease of making: 3
- Time to make: 45 minutes
- Expandable length: 300–400 (12–15¾in) plus 40mm (1½in) drop

Everyone loves a rainbow because its beautiful colours are a joy to behold, so what better than a necklace that echoes this wonderful effect of nature? Once again, the crystal beads are from Swarovski and their perfection and sparkle are ideal for this fun jewellery item. The range of colours available is huge, and here I have chosen those of a subtle hue more in keeping with nature. The smallest beads are faceted sterling silver and the larger ones are silver-plated pewter, giving an overall high-quality finish.

The necklace is threaded onto memory wire, which, as its name suggests, 'remembers' its shape, so that when cut into lengths and pulled apart, it instantly springs back to its original circular shape (see page 13). It can be used to make single-strand, as here, or multi-strand jewellery.

So, get beading and you can have a rainbow without a single drop of rain!

INGREDIENTS

- 3 Swarovski crystal bicone beads, 4mm, in each of the following colours: Tanzanite, Light Amethyst, Paparadscha, Topaz, Colorado Topaz, Erinite and Sapphire
- 1 Swarovski crystal bicone bead, 5mm, in each of the colours above
- 1 Swarovski crystal bicone bead, 6mm, in each of the colours above
- 85 sterling silver faceted beads, 2mm
- 22 silver-plated faceted bicone beads, 4mm
- 7 'gold' headpins, 75mm
- 2 'silver' memory wire end beads, 5mm
- 1½ coils of necklace-length memory wire
- gel superglue

1 Apply a very small amount of gel superglue to one end of the memory wire and then fit one of the 'silver' memory wire end beads onto this end. After removing surplus glue with a tissue, leave to dry while you make the drops.

2 Refer to the photograph for the threading sequence to make up the drops, using the headpins and following the instructions for Basic Earring Making, page 18. Make sure that the drops are evenly graduated in length.

3 Referring to the photograph, thread onto the memory wire the sequence of beads for one side of the choker, followed by the drops and then the remaining beads. Be careful while doing this as the cut end of the memory wire will be very sharp.

4 Repeat Step 1 to attach the other memory wire end bead to the other end of the choker.

Blue Ice Choker

- Ease of making: 2
- Time to make: 15 minutes
- Length: 400mm (15¾in)

Looking just like a chunk of shining ice, this polished quartz crystal defies its cold appearance with a highly tactile quality. It is a beautifully simple object and to embellish it with too many other beads would be a shame, so I have chosen to make a cord from which to suspend it and only added two textured silvery beads for contrast. The cord is made by combining three colours of embroidery cottons (floss) into a twisted rope. This is a medium and method that I like, as embroidery threads are made in hundreds of colours from which you can choose any combination to make a cord that fits your requirements exactly. The cottons (floss) can be twisted by hand or, for speed, you may wish to use the spinster tool – see page 15.

INGREDIENTS

- 1 polished quartz crystal, 25–28mm
- 2 'silver' beads, 8mm
- 2 'silver' square calotte crimps
- 1 'silver' hook clasp
- 3 x 1m (39in) lengths of embroidery cotton (floss) in different colours

Follow Steps 1–4 for Flora, page 67, to make the cord, and attach the square calotte crimps and clasp to the cord following the instructions for Making a Thong, page 18. Refer to the photograph for the design, making simple overhand knots in the cord where shown.

Crystal Tears

- Ease of making: 3
- Time to make: 10 minutes
- Length: 50mm (2in)

The focal beads of these earrings are Czech glass, which are chunkier and less sparkly than those used in the previous project, but the effect is that of cut rock crystal and the overall result is very wearable and much less expensive. The ear-hooks are among the cheapest available, but as they originate from within the EU, they comply with the recent nickel regulations and should not give rise to allergy problems (see page 12). However, like all of the lower-priced plated metals, the bright metallic finish will eventually disappear and the metal will appear tarnished. If you are making fashion earrings, with a short life expectancy, this may be acceptable, but I believe that good-quality beads deserve findings to match, so elsewhere in the book those that I use are in general the best that I have been able to find.

INGREDIENTS

- 2 faceted teardrop beads, 13 x 9mm
- 2 silver-plated floral links
- 4 bead caps, 3mm
- 2 silver-plated headpins, 50mm
- 2 silver-plated ear-hooks

Refer to the photograph for the design and make up the earrings following the instructions for Basic Earring Making, page 18.

BUGLES AND ROCAILLES

The bugle is a useful little bead. It is made from a long glass tube that is heated, stretched and, when at the required thickness, cut into lengths (see page 8). A wide range of colours, as well as sizes, is available and the bead is useful in all sorts of beading applications, from jewellery to beaded lampshades. In the two projects that follow I have used bugles almost exclusively, but often, like their rocaille 'cousins' in the following projects, they appear almost unnoticed as the unsung 'backing chorus' to the main event.

Rocailles are made in a similar process to bugles, but the range of colour and size is even greater, and if you are looking for beads to colour-match an outfit, you are almost certain to find something that fits the bill in rocailles. There are also many types of finish available, including oily and AB-coated featured in this section (see page 8). The quality varies enormously too, from tiny and perfectly matched to 5mm, unevenly sized beads. Like bugles, rocailles are often simply used as spacers between larger beads in jewellery and you will see many examples of such use throughout the book, but here I have chosen a few designs to use them in a more creative way, in order to free your imagination.

Peacock Tail Set

├─ Ease of making: Necklace 10; Earrings 4
├─ Time to make: Necklace 9 hours; Earrings 45 minutes
└─ Length: Necklace 350–400mm (13¾–15¾in) plus 70mm (2¾in) drop; Earrings 100mm (4in)

The cost of making this necklace is among the lowest in the book, but in terms of patience and dexterity it is one of the most challenging! The beads are reminiscent of the iridescence of a peacock's tail, and the overall effect is stunning. Each individual will prefer a particular position where the necklace sits on the neck, so a simple chain and-hook fastener gives multiple lengths. As this necklace is likely to be worn with party clothes, I have added beaded droppers to hang elegantly from the nape of the neck. A matching pair of earrings can be made by following Step 12 for the threading sequence and the instructions for Tailor-making Ear-hooks, page 19, for the ear-hooks. Generally, I do not give amounts for bugles or rocailles in the project 'ingredient' lists, but here I have listed the approximate quantities required (including for the earrings), although these beads are purchased by weight or packet size rather than quantity.

INGREDIENTS

- 220 oily-finish green/black twisted bugles, 10mm
- 60 'gold'-lined faceted bugles, 7mm
- 900 oily-finish blue/black faceted bugles, 2mm
- 600 medium 'gold' rocailles
- 2 small rocailles
- 45mm (1¾in) length of 'gold' heavyweight curb chain
- 70mm (2¾in) length of 'gold' heavyweight curb chain
- 4 'gold' calottes
- 1 'gold' hook clasp
- 6m (6½yd) length of fine monofilament nylon beading thread
- flexible twisted wire beading needle (optional)

1 Cut two 1m (39in) lengths of nylon thread and tie one end of each length to a small rocaille. Thread the free end of each nylon thread through the hole of a calotte and pull the bead and knot down into the 'shell' of the calotte (diagram A). Trim any excess thread and use flat-nosed or general-purpose pliers to squeeze the calotte closed.

A

2 Thread four 2mm faceted bugles onto each length of nylon thread.

3 Thread a 10mm bugle onto one length of nylon thread, then pass the other length through this bugle from the opposite direction (diagram B). Continue threading on 10mm bugles in this way until you have threaded about 146 bugles. During the process of threading, you will need to add extra lengths of thread several times. Attach the additional thread by knotting it onto the existing thread in as unobtrusive way as possible (diagram C). Finish by repeating Steps 1–2 in reverse order, but leave the second calotte open at this stage.

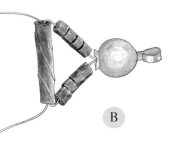

B

C

4 Take a new 1m (39in) length of nylon beading thread and tie one end around the rocaille that is inside the open calotte. Trim the spare nylon thread. Use flat-nosed or general-purpose pliers to close the calotte. Pass the thread through one set of four 2mm faceted bugles threaded on in Step 2.

5 Thread one 'gold' rocaille onto the nylon thread and then pass the thread down through the first bugle.

6 Thread two 'gold' rocailles onto the nylon thread and then pass the thread up through the next bugle. Continue working in this way until you have threaded through 50 bugles.

7 Thread down through the next bugle and thread on one rocaille, then thread on one 2mm bugle, one 7mm bugle, one 2mm bugle, one rocaille, one 10mm bugle and four rocailles (diagram D).

8 Now thread back up through the first threaded bead of the last four rocailles and all the other beads in Step 7. When the nylon thread emerges at the top of the last bugle, thread on one more rocaille and then thread down through the adjacent bugle and thread on the same sequence of beads as in Step 7, but instead of threading one 2mm bugle at the beginning of the drop, thread two 2mm bugles (diagram D).

9 Continue in this way to form 25 drops, adding an extra 2mm bugle with every drop threaded.

10 After 25 drops have been made, continue forming drops in the same way, but decrease the number of 2mm bugles by one for each drop. After 24 more drops, repeat Step 6 to complete the threading.

D

11 Attach one length of chain to each of the calottes at the ends of the necklace by using flat-nosed or general-purpose pliers to open and then close the loops of the calottes.

12 Make one of the drops for hanging at the back of the necklace by tying a 500mm (20in) length of nylon thread to a small rocaille, then pass the thread down through the hole of a calotte. Thread the nylon thread with beads, referring to the photograph on page 49 for the threading sequence. Omitting the last three rocailles, thread back up through the beads just threaded, through the calotte and also the rocaille.

Continuing with the same thread, go back down through the calotte and repeat the first drop made, but finishing at a different length. Repeat once more to make the last of the three drops and finish by threading up through the calotte and securely tying the nylon thread to the rocaille. Trim the excess thread and use pliers as before to squeeze the calotte closed.

13 Repeat Step 12 to make the second group of beaded drops and then attach these to each end of the chain and the hook clasp to a suitable point along the chain.

Silver Streak

└ Ease of making: 3
└ Time to make: 30 minutes
└ Length: 120mm (4¾in)

Absolute simplicity and free movement make these elegant lightweight earrings a joy to make and wear, and they are sure to raise many compliments. Even though all the metal components are sterling silver, they are inexpensive to make. However, if you want to cut costs further, you could use silver-plated ear-hooks and 2mm beads instead to the same effect.

INGREDIENTS

◎ 22 sterling silver faceted beads, 2mm
◎ 10 'silver'-lined bugles, 20mm
◎ 2 sterling silver coils, 2mm
◎ 10 sterling silver headpins
◎ 2 sterling silver jump rings, 5mm
◎ 4 sterling silver jump rings, 4mm
◎ 2 sterling silver straight-leg angular ear-hooks

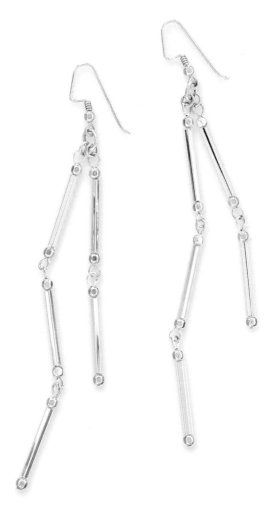

To make up the earrings, refer to the photograph for the design and follow the instructions for Basic Earring Making, page 18.

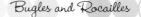

Turquoise Fans

- Ease of making: 7
- Time to make: 4 hours
- Length: 420mm (16½in) plus 70mm (2¾in) drop

There are few items in this book that I have specifically designed for myself, but this is one, and I chose the colours to suit a black dress with turquoise edging – the result was perfection! The run of the beads within the drops is haphazard and this means that you can rummage through your bead box to find 'odds and ends' to match your background rocailles.

Three different threading mediums are used: the drops are threaded on fine, coloured wire, and these are suspended from a short length of memory wire, used to give a consistent curve to the front of the necklace, while the remainder is nylon-coated wire.

INGREDIENTS
- small 'silver'-lined rocailles
- small oily-finish dark blue rocailles
- about 60 large rocailles in complementary colours
- about 15 other beads in complementary colours, 4–5mm
- 2 beads in complementary colours, 6–7mm
- 3 'gold' beads, 4–6mm
- 1 bead in a complementary colour, 8mm
- a few small 'gold'-lined rocailles
- 4 goldfill crimp beads
- 1 toggle clasp
- 100mm (4in) length of memory wire
- 2 x 200mm (8in) lengths of nylon-coated wire
- 2m (79in) fine jewellery wire in a matching colour

1 Use round-nosed pliers to form a loop at one end of the length of memory wire, working gradually rather than in one motion.

2 Thread 42 small rocailles in a random sequence of two colours onto the wire, then use the round-nosed pliers to form another loop at the other end of the memory wire.

3 Count 13 beads in from one loop and push one end of the length of fine jewellery wire under the rocailles, then twist the wire around the memory wire a few times to secure. Thread about six beads in a random sequence onto the jewellery wire, finishing with a relatively large bead. Now thread the wire back up through the first five beads.

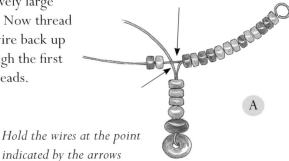

A

Hold the wires at the point indicated by the arrows

4 With your finger and thumb, hold the jewellery wire and memory wire as shown in diagram A (opposite) and use your other hand to twist the bottom bead until the wire is twisted all along its length. As this is coloured jewellery wire, it is a matter of preference whether or not you leave the twisted wire showing, as I have here.

5 Wind the jewellery wire around the memory wire once or twice, then pass the wire over the next rocaille on the memory wire. Following Steps 3–4, make another twisted wire beaded drop using ten beads. Make a total of nine drops of increasing length, then gradually decrease the length of the drops until the second side of the necklace matches the first. Twist the jewellery wire around the memory wire and tuck the end beneath some of the rocailles on the memory wire.

6 Make the two sides of the necklace using the nylon-coated wire, rocailles and crimp beads, following the instructions for Simple Necklace Stringing, page 16, and attaching one end of each section to one part of the clasp. Attach each of the other ends to a loop of the memory wire.

To make up the earrings, follow Steps 3–4 to form the beaded drops in varying lengths (ignoring the memory wire) and leave enough wire at the beginning and end of threading. At the end of threading, use the spare wire to catch up all the wire at the top of the middle two drops, then twist together and use to form a loop for attachment to the ear-hooks.

Time to Bead

Ease of making: 5
Time to make: 2 hours
Length: 190mm (7½in)

Today, there is a huge variety of fashion watches to be found in shopping malls around the world and we have all become used to colourful time pieces, so what better than to make one for yourself? Many bead suppliers keep stocks of watches purpose made for beading, usually with three holes ready for applying a beaded bracelet.

INGREDIENTS

◎ medium rocailles (those featured here are blue/mauve AB-coated)
◎ 12 gold-plated faceted bicone beads, 3mm
◎ 2 'gold' jump rings, 5mm
◎ 6 'gold' crimp beads
◎ 6 x 8mm (³/₈in) lengths of 'gold' gimp
◎ 1 watch with 3 holes
◎ 2 gold-plated 3–1 bracelet/necklace ends
◎ 1 gold-plated toggle clasp
◎ 4 x 200mm (8in) lengths of nylon-coated wire
◎ 2 x 100mm (4in) lengths of nylon-coated wire

1 Thread a crimp bead onto each of two 200mm (8in) and one 100mm (4in) lengths of nylon-coated wire, then thread the wire back through the crimp to make a tiny loop. Trim the excess wire close to the loop (diagram A). This ensures that there are no sharp ends of wire to stick into the skin.

A

2 Thread each longer length of wire through an outer hole and the shorter length of wire through the middle hole provided in the watch, with the crimp beads concealed from view at the back of the watch.

3 Thread eight rocailles onto one of the longer lengths of wire and four rocailles onto the other longer length of wire. Then thread the wire with four beads through the last four beads threaded on the first length of wire (diagram B).

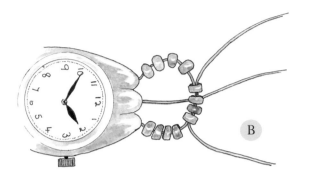

B

4 Thread onto the shorter length of wire one rocaille, a faceted bicone and another rocaille. Thread the wire between the longer wires in the middle of the four beads through which both long wires pass (diagram C).

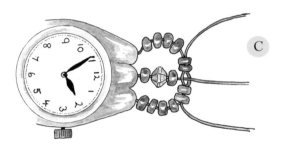

C

5 Repeat Steps 3–4 five more times, or until the watch bracelet is the required length. Thread one rocaille onto each wire, then attach each wire to one of the holes in one of the bracelet/necklace ends, using a length of gimp and a crimp bead and following the instructions for Simple Necklace Stringing, page 16.

6 Repeat Steps 1–5 to make the other side of the watch bracelet. Use jump rings to attach the toggle clasp to the necklace ends, opening them sideways using flat-nosed or general-purpose pliers.

From the Deep

- Ease of making: 5
- Time to make: 4 hours
- Length: 500mm (20in) plus 150mm (6in) drop

And now for something completely different! When I first saw this slice of telescopium shell, a necklace sprang to mind, but I put off making it as I was undecided about what beads to use and how to approach the design. After much deliberation and several false starts it finally started to fall into place, although I was still unsure and felt I might be making something I would dislike. Several hours later the result was the necklace that you see here and I was pleasantly surprised by the effect, which reminds me of an exotic deep-sea creature.

Shell slices such as this are inexpensive and can be found in the catalogues of bead suppliers. The rocailles have been chosen to match the natural colours of the shell. The beads and small drops at the end of each hanging thread are all gold-plated pewter and are fairly heavy, so they hang well.

INGREDIENTS

- 1 telescopium shell slice
- 3 quantities of small rocailles in different toning autumn colours
- 8 gold-plated faceted bicone beads, 3mm
- 1 gold-plated tube-shaped bead, 14 x 4mm
- 6 gold-plated pendant drops
- 1 goldfill bead, 2mm
- 21 goldfill crimp beads
- 2 gold-plated 3–1 necklace ends
- 1 'gold' hook clasp
- 6 x 300mm (12in) lengths of 'bronze' fine nylon-coated wire
- 3 x 210mm (8¼in) lengths of 'bronze' fine nylon-coated wire

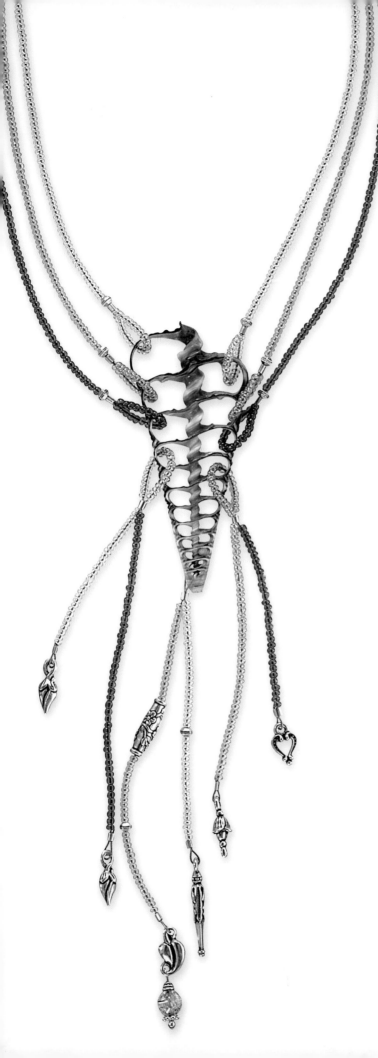

1 Attach one 300m (12in) length of nylon-coated wire to an outer loop of one of the 3–1 necklace ends, using a crimp bead and following the instructions for Simple Necklace Stringing, page 16. Thread on about 200mm (8in) of the palest-coloured rocailles, then thread on one 3mm faceted bicone bead and a crimp bead. Thread on another 30mm (1in) of the pale rocailles and pass this length through the top hole of one side of the telescopium shell, making a loop to secure the beads around the shell. Thread the wire back through the crimp bead and use crimp or general-purpose pliers to secure the crimp in place.

2 Repeat Step 1 twice more on the same side of the shell, using medium-coloured rocailles for the second and darker-coloured rocailles for the third and increasing the main length of threaded rocailles each time to suit the graduation of the shell.

3 Repeat Steps 1–2 for the other side of the necklace, but because the shell is a product of nature, the holes will not be regularly spaced, so you will need to vary the lengths of threaded rocailles accordingly to make the necklace hang correctly.

4 Attach one 210mm (8¼in) length of nylon-coated wire to a pendant drop, using a crimp bead and following the instructions for Simple Necklace Stringing, page 16. Thread on about 60mm (2½in) of rocailles, then thread on a crimp bead and about another 30mm (1in) of rocailles. Pass this beaded section through another hole in the shell, forming a loop, and thread the wire back through the crimp bead, as shown in the photograph. Thread on about 50mm (2in) of rocailles in a different colour. Finish in the same way as for the beginning of this step, attaching another gold-plated drop.

5 Repeat Step 4 twice to make and attach the other beaded drops to the shell, staggering the lengths of the beaded drops and interspersing the remaining gold beads in the rocailles of the middle lower drop, as seen in the photograph.

6 Attach the hook clasp to one of the 3–1 necklace ends to complete the necklace.

PRECIOUS PEARLS

Man must have prized the pearl since he started eating oysters and discovered their secret treasure. And no wonder, for each pearl is an object of great beauty. A natural pearl owes its origins to a humble grain of sand (or other irritant) beneath the oyster shell. The oyster lays coatings of nacre (pearlized shell) over the foreign body to render it smooth; thus the pearl is 'born', and the longer it remains within the shell, the larger it grows. An artificial irritant can be introduced to produce the cultivated pearl, although this remains an expensive product. Freshwater mussels also form pearls and these too are now 'farmed'. Trends in fashion have led to a much greater production of cultivated freshwater pearls, so today they are available in a huge range of sizes, shapes and colours. They are also relatively inexpensive, so now pearls with a true lustre are available to all. But if you really need to tailor your jewellery to your pocket, turn to artificial pearls, which offer a wide choice in quality and therefore price, and are available in an even greater colour range than real pearls.

Modern Tradition

Ease of making: 6
Time to make: 1½ hours
Length: 430mm (17in)

The classic pearl necklace is always knotted, giving security (if your necklace breaks, you will lose just one bead at most) and an unsurpassed drape. As the thread is visible, it usually matches the bead colour. But this freshwater pearl necklace has a modern edge, with a toning thread colour to enhance the natural creaminess of the beads. These cultivated pearls have a beautiful lustre, shown off by their relatively large size. Like all pearls, they are normally sold by the 450mm (17¾in) string.

I have used my own knotting method, using a single thread, developed because the holes in freshwater pearls are often exceedingly small and it can be very difficult to pass two threads through. (This method can be used for threading any beads.) You may need a bead reamer (see page 15) to enlarge the holes, although I did not need one here. The instructions assume that you are using your thread with a flexible twisted wire beading needle, but you could use beading silk with its needle attached (available from bead suppliers).

INGREDIENTS

- 30 freshwater pearls, 12 x 8mm
- 2 goldfill crimp beads
- 2 x 8mm (³/₈in) lengths of 'gold' gimp
- 1 gold-plated toggle clasp
- 120cm (47in) length of thread
- flexible twisted wire beading needle
- gel superglue

1 Thread one length of gimp onto the end of the thread, leaving about 100mm (4in) free, and then pass this through the loop of the clasp. With the loose end, tie an overhand knot to loop around the thread close to the other end of the gimp (diagram A). The gimp behind this knot will help to back it up and prevent the bead slipping over it.

A

2 Thread on one bead and, if the bead hole is large enough, the spare length of thread too. Tie another overhand knot over the main thread and close to the

bead. Using sharp scissors, trim the loose thread neatly and for additional security apply a tiny touch of gel superglue to seal the last knot (if any of this touches your bead it will be spoilt, so apply very carefully with something like a headpin). If it was not possible to thread the spare thread through the first bead, tie another knot over the first one for security, then trim the spare thread and seal with a tiny amount of superglue as above.

3 Thread on another bead, and tie your knot as follows (diagrams B–F):

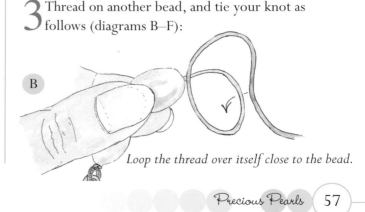

B

Loop the thread over itself close to the bead.

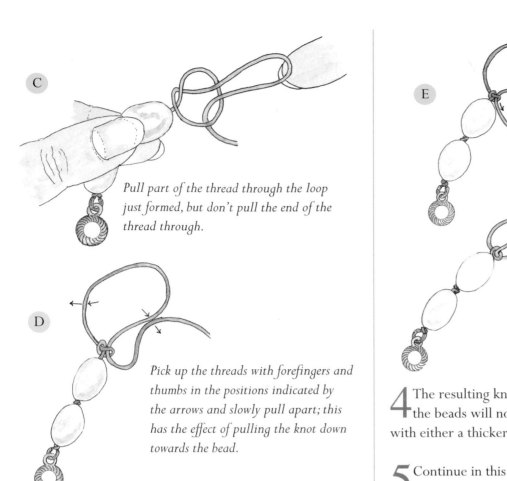

C

Pull part of the thread through the loop just formed, but don't pull the end of the thread through.

D

Pick up the threads with forefingers and thumbs in the positions indicated by the arrows and slowly pull apart; this has the effect of pulling the knot down towards the bead.

When you are satisfied that the knot is tight up to the bead, pass the loose end of thread through the loop.

E

Gently pull the thread through the loop, but be careful to do this slowly or the thread will twist.

F

4 The resulting knot should be sufficiently large that the beads will not slide over it. If they do, start again with either a thicker or doubled thread.

5 Continue in this way until your necklace is the required length. Finish by attaching the thread to the clasp, trimming and gluing it, as in Steps 1–2.

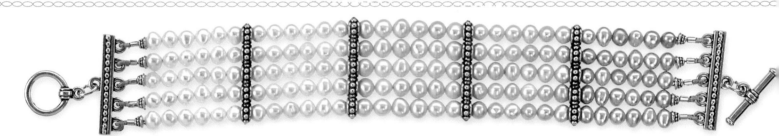

Pearl Cuff Bracelet

Ease of making: 4
Time to make: 3 hours
Length: 200mm (8in)

This bracelet has the look and feel of quality. The lustrous freshwater pearls have a pleasing uniformity of shape and size, and are threaded in blocks of colour to show something of the wide range of shades available. I took these pearls from a ready-made necklace purchased only for the beads – freshwater pearls are often exported as ready-made items of jewellery, and such necklaces contain a large number of good-quality pearls. Keep your eyes open for similar bargains when browsing in gift shops. The necklace that I found was a string of beaded 'beads' (i.e. small beads strung together to make a larger 'bead'), as used in the Fleur Earrings below. These are available from some bead suppliers, but if you are dexterous, you might like to produce your own! It can be tricky to ensure that all the threads finish at exactly the same length, but the method really is as simple as the basic technique, so refer to this in addition to the instructions below.

INGREDIENTS

◉ 30 potato (oval) freshwater pearls, 5 x 4mm, in 5 different colours
◉ 10 gold-plated bead caps, 4mm
◉ 4 gold-plated 5-hole spacer bars
◉ 2 'gold' jump rings
◉ 10 goldfill crimp beads
◉ 5 inexpensive crimp beads for use as temporary 'stoppers'
◉ 10 x 8mm (³/₈in) lengths of 'gold' gimp
◉ 2 gold-plated 5–1 necklace/bracelet ends
◉ 1 gold-plated toggle clasp
◉ 5 x 300mm (12in) lengths of white fine nylon-coated wire

1 Attach the five lengths of nylon-coated wire to the loops of one of the 5–1 necklace/bracelet ends using goldfill crimp beads and gimp, following the instructions for Simple Necklace Stringing, page 16.

2 Thread one bead cap and six pearls onto one thread and then thread on one of the spacer bars through the appropriate hole.

3 Thread on six more pearls, but this time choosing a different colour.

4 Omitting the bead cap, repeat Steps 2–3 until the end of the bracelet, finishing with one bead cap. Then thread through the appropriate loop of the other necklace/bracelet end. Do not fasten the thread at this point, but apply an inexpensive crimp to the end of the thread to act as a temporary 'stopper'.

5 Thread the remaining four lengths of wire as above, then cut off the temporary crimp beads, thread each wire with gimp and a goldfill crimp bead and adjust the lengths to match each other. Squeeze the crimp beads onto the thread and trim the wire ends (diagram A).

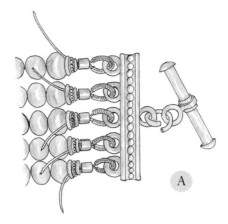

A

6 Attach each part of the toggle clasp to one necklace/bracelet end with a jump ring, using flat-nosed or general-purpose pliers to open the jump ring sideways (diagram A).

Fleur Earrings

⌐ Ease of making: 3
⌐ Time to make: 15 minutes
⌐ Length: 45mm (1¾in)

As mentioned in Pearl Cuff Bracelet, the feature beads of this pair of earrings came pre-strung on a long necklace that I simply dismantled for its components. On a whole necklace these beaded pearl beads were over-ornate, but just one per earring looks good, especially for party wear. To complement the dressy look I have chosen a beautiful pair of fleur-de-lys ear-studs made from gold-plated pewter. The earrings are simple to make – just refer to the photograph for the design and follow the instructions for Basic Earring Making, page 18, for the method.

Midnight Pearl Choker

Ease of making: 3
Time to make: 1½ hours
Length: 430–490mm (17–19¼in)

Although the colour of these pearls is not natural, they are a wonderfully lustrous rich bronze, and together, the necklace and earrings look a million dollars! The overall effect is simple, but the pearl-loop back drop lends a touch of elegance. The necklace uses the same method as Pearl Cuff Bracelet, page 58, so it is not difficult to make. I did have some difficulty in designing it so that the lower strand drapes correctly, just below the higher one, but if you are using beads of the same size as these, the threading sequence as shown in the photograph will work well. There is no exact formula for achieving this, so if you use beads of a different size, you should try the necklace on before finally fixing the clasp.

Follow Steps 1–4 of Pearl Cuff Bracelet, but ignore that sequence of threading and instead refer to the photograph. The instructions below are for the loop at the back of the necklace.

INGREDIENTS

- 2 x 450mm (17¾in) strings of 6 x 5mm potato (oval) freshwater pearls
- 22 gold-plated beaded rondels, 5mm
- 5 gold-plated bead caps, 4mm
- 4 gold-plated 2 hole spacer bars, 10mm
- 1 'gold' necklace end cap, 3mm
- 4 large 'bronze' rocailles
- 5 goldfill crimp beads
- 5 x 8mm (³/8in) lengths of 'gold' gimp
- 70mm (2¾in) length of 'gold' chain
- 2 gold-plated 2–1 necklace ends, 10mm
- 1 'gold' hook clasp
- 2 x 500mm (20in) lengths of 'bronze' fine nylon-coated wire
- 100mm (4in) length of 'bronze' fine nylon-coated wire

1 Use flat-nosed or general-purpose pliers to open and attach two links to one of the necklace ends and then add the hook clasp, referring to diagram D for Disco Choker on page 86.

2 Attach the remainder of the chain to the other necklace end as above.

3 Using the 100mm (4in) length of wire, thread on the pearls and beaded rondels in the sequence as shown, beginning and ending with one of the 'bronze' rocailles.

4 Thread both ends through a bead cap and then a goldfill crimp bead. Ensuring that there is no slack thread in the beaded loop, use crimp pliers to squeeze the crimp closed over the two wires.

5 Use sharp cutting pliers to trim one length of wire as close to the crimp as possible. Thread onto the remaining wire the necklace end cap, a crimp bead and a length of gimp (diagram A).

6 Thread the wire end through the last link of the longer length of chain, then back through the crimp bead and the necklace end cap (diagram A). Pull the thread through to form a neat loop and secure the beaded loop to the chain by squeezing the crimp bead onto the wire. Trim this thread with the point of a pair of cutting pliers so that the end will be hidden beneath the necklace end cap.

A

Midnight Pearl Earrings

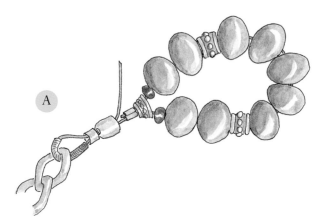

— Ease of making: 3
— Time to make: 15 minutes
— Length: 50mm (2in)

So, you have made the necklace – what better now than a matching pair of simply made earrings to use a few leftover beads?

INGREDIENTS
◎ 4 potato (oval) freshwater pearls, 6 x 5mm
◎ 8 goldfill beads, 2mm
◎ 4 gold-plated bead caps, 4mm
◎ 4 plain 'gold' washer beads
◎ 2 goldfill beads, 3mm
◎ 2 goldfill coils, 3mm
◎ 10 goldfill crimp beads
◎ 2 goldfill straight-leg angular ear-hooks
◎ 2 x 80mm (3¼in) lengths of 'bronze' fine nylon-coated wire

1 Make up the ear-hooks, following the instructions for Tailor-making Ear-hooks, page 19.

2 Thread a crimp bead onto one length of wire and use crimp pliers to squeeze it onto the wire close to one end. Refer to the photograph to thread on beads for one drop.

3 Thread on another crimp bead, thread the unthreaded end of the wire back through that crimp

and adjust the wire so that the beaded drop hangs at about 25mm (1in). Pull the wire to form a small loop (diagram A), then use crimp pliers to squeeze the crimp onto the wire and secure the loop.

4 Thread the unthreaded length with the same sequence of beads but in reverse order so that the second drop matches the first one. Thread on the last crimp and adjust the length of the drop to about 35mm (1¼in). Squeeze the crimp bead onto the wire.

A

5 Attach the drops to the ear-hook. Using sharp cutting pliers, trim the excess wire on the drops as close to the crimp bead as possible. Repeat Steps 2–5 to make the other earring.

Pearl's a Swinger

- Ease of making: 3
- Time to make: 45 minutes
- Length: 410mm (16¼in) plus 60mm (2½in) pendant

INGREDIENTS

◎ 29 freshwater pearls, 4mm
◎ 1 freshwater pearl, 6mm
◎ 1 small 'gold' rocaille
◎ 4 gold-plated bead caps, 4mm
◎ 1 gold-plated beaded rondel, 4mm
◎ 1 gold-plated 5–1 fan-shaped necklace end
◎ 2 'gold' square calotte crimps
◎ 3 gold-plated jump rings
◎ 6 goldfill crimp beads
◎ 1 gold-plated clasp
◎ 330mm (13in) length of nylon-coated wire
◎ 500mm (20in) length of rat-tail

Sometimes when making a necklace just a few beads get left over. Here is a great idea for using them. Just a few special beads are all you need to form the focus of a pendant. The gold fan that I have chosen as the base for this pendant is a useful item and could equally well be utilized in earrings or as a 5–1 necklace end. The pendant is quite simple to make using the skills learned in the previous two projects.

1 Thread a crimp bead onto a 50mm (2in) length of nylon-coated wire and use crimp pliers to squeeze it onto one end. Refer to the photographs to thread the central drop. Attach the wire to the central hole in the necklace end using a crimp bead without gimp, following the instructions for Simple Necklace Stringing, page 16. Trim the excess wire at both ends.

2 Cut a 130mm (5in) length of wire and attach it to the hole next to the central one in the pendant, as in Step 1. Thread on beads in the sequence as shown and when finished attach the wire to the matching hole on the other side of the pendant, again as in Step 1.

3 Cut a 150mm (6in) length of wire. Again, refer to the photographs for the threading sequence and follow Step 1 to attach to the outside pendant holes.

4 Attach a calotte crimp to either end of the rat-tail and use jump rings to attach it to the clasp, following the instructions for Making a Thong Necklace, page 18. Use a jump ring to attach the pendant to the length of rat-tail.

Moonlight Drops Necklace

—Ease of making: 4

—Time to make: 1½ hours

—Length: 400mm (15¾in) plus 100mm (4in) drop

INGREDIENTS

- ◎ 450mm (17¾in) string of 12mm disc-shaped freshwater pearls
- ◎ 450mm (17¾in) string of 5 x 4mm potato (oval) freshwater pearls
- ◎ 16 gold-plated bead caps, 4mm
- ◎ 16 small 'gold' crimp beads
- ◎ 2 x 8mm (³/₈in) lengths of gimp
- ◎ 1 gold-plated clasp set with glass pearls
- ◎ 900mm (35in) length of fine nylon-coated wire

1 Make up the drops referring to the photograph for the threading sequence and following Steps 2–3 of Midnight Pearl Earrings, page 61, but using the small 'gold' crimp beads.

2 After forming the loop and squeezing the crimp onto the wire, trim the wire as close as possible to the crimp and from the bottom of the drop.

3 Cut a 460mm (18in) length of wire and use gimp and a crimp bead to attach it to one part of the clasp, following the instructions for Simple Necklace Stringing, page 16. Thread on 40 potato pearls, then the shortest drop, three more pearls and the next drop.

4 Following the sequence in the photograph, continue threading beads and drops until complete. Repeat Step 3 to attach the other part of the clasp.

This striking necklace calls for a special occasion and already a friend has earmarked it for her next cruise! The colour of the beads is natural, and because the disc beads are large, they exhibit a beautiful sheen with a look of moonlit iridescence. Their shape, however, quite obviously owes little to nature! Both types of bead are available in other colours. Flat beads are also available in square and diamond shapes, so you could make a necklace using the same design but with a completely different appearance.

Versatility

Ease of making: 2
Time to make: 1¼ hours
Length: 1m (39in)

This necklace features glass pearls, from the quality end of the range of artificial pearls on offer. More sophisticated varieties of glass bead offer UV light-, alkali- and perspiration-resistant lustrous coatings, which are obviously more expensive, but if you want your jewellery item to last, the extra outlay is worthwhile.

For versatility this necklace is hard to beat as it can be worn as a choker, mid-length or as a long necklace. It is also easy to make, although you will experience a little threading difficulty with the particular pearls that I have chosen due to their small holes. However, you could use any pearls or indeed any bead to make a necklace in the same style but with a different look.

INGREDIENTS

- 186 glass pearls, 4mm
- 84 matt-finish 'gold' beads, 3mm
- 116 small matt-finish mauve rocailles
- 2 gold-plated pendant drops
- 3 'gold' crimp beads
- 1 inexpensive crimp bead for use as a temporary 'stopper'
- 110cm (43in) length of white fine nylon-coated wire
- 130mm (5in) length of white fine nylon-coated wire

1 Attach one pendant drop to the longer length of nylon-coated wire using a crimp bead without gimp, following the instructions for Simple Necklace Stringing, page 16. Refer to the photograph to thread on the beads and then attach another pendant drop to the end of the wire as before.

2 Make up the 'knot' by attaching a crimp bead as a temporary 'stopper' to the end of the shorter length of nylon-coated wire, then thread on 16 matt-finish 'gold' beads. Pass the thread back through the third bead threaded to form a circle, leaving 10mm (½in) of spare wire (diagram A).

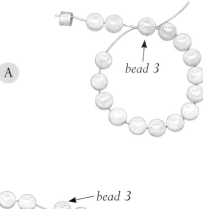

A   bead 3

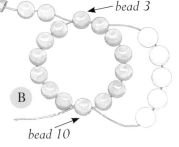

B   bead 3

bead 10

3 Thread on five pearls and then pass the thread through the tenth bead from the crimp bead (diagram B). Thread on five more pearls and then thread through the third bead again.

4 Thread on six matt-finish 'gold' beads, then again thread through the tenth bead of the circle.

5 Thread on four matt-finish 'gold' beads and a crimp bead. Cut off the first temporary crimp bead from the other end of the

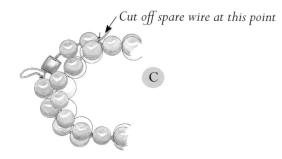

Cut off spare wire at this point

C

wire and thread this spare wire through the crimp bead and through one or two of the 'gold' beads (diagram C). Thread the spare wire at the other end through the crimp bead and one or two of the 'gold' beads and then pull both ends to ensure as little slack in the thread and as tight a knot as possible. Secure everything in place by using flat-nosed or general-purpose pliers to squeeze the crimp bead onto the wire.

Golden Wedding

Ease of making: 3
Time to make: 45 minutes
Length: 200mm (8in)

Wouldn't this make a perfect gift for a 50th wedding anniversary? The bracelet is made from 'gold' Czech glass pearls and the spacers and clasps are gold-plated pewter. The whole effect and feel of the finished item is of quality, although the cost of making it is low. Like so many other projects in this book, you should consider making up this design in other beads for an alternative effect. For instance, it could be made with any 8mm glass beads to match a particular outfit or with traditional white or cream pearls to go with a wedding dress, and just doubling up on the quantities would provide enough components for a beautiful choker.

INGREDIENTS

◎ 36 'gold' pearls, 8mm
◎ 5 gold-plated cube-shaped beads, 6mm
◎ 4 gold-plated bead caps, 4mm
◎ 5 'gold' headpins, 50mm
◎ 2 'gold' jump rings
◎ 4 goldfill crimp beads
◎ 2 gold-plated 2–1 necklace/bracelet ends
◎ 1 gold-plated clasp
◎ 2 x 250mm (10in) lengths of 'bronze' nylon-coated wire

1 Make up one of the connectors for the bracelet by cutting the head off a headpin and making a loop, following Steps 3 and 5 of Basic Earring Making, page 18. Thread on one of the gold-plated cube-shaped beads and then, after cutting off the excess headpin wire, make another loop. Be sure to make both loops in the same direction (diagram A). Repeat this procedure with all the other cube beads and headpins.

2 Attach each length of nylon-coated wire to a hole in one of the necklace/bracelet

A

ends using a crimp bead and following the instructions for Simple Necklace Stringing, page 16. Referring to the photograph for the design, thread the beads and connectors onto the wires. Attach the wires to the other necklace/bracelet end as before. Use a jump ring to attach each part of the clasp to a necklace/bracelet end, opening the jump ring sideways with flat-nosed or general-purpose pliers.

DESIGNER GALLERY

A round the world bead artists are proliferating, so bead lovers now have a much greater choice of individual handmade items. Many of these artists, passionate about their work, are developing techniques to bring us exciting and innovative new beads. Some such beads are expensive one-offs. Others are more affordable and available, being made to a more standard design while retaining high handmade quality, with individual quirks and differences. Some of my favourites from England, Germany and America are shown in this section, although a quick Internet search will reveal many other beads of stunning beauty and design. Because I love these beads so much, I want to show you a wide variety and various simple ways of using such individual items.

Flora

- Ease of making: 4
- Time to make: 45 minutes
- Length: 660mm (26in)

For this necklace, I have strung together some beautiful large lamp beads from Tuffnell Glass of Yorkshire, England (see page 126), each one incorporating several colours in beautiful three-dimensional floral designs. With beads of such intricacy and weight, I have kept the design simple to make a long necklace to slip over the head and wear draped over a plain sweater. Handmade from embroidery cotton (floss), the cord can be matched to any range of bead colours of your choice.

1 Double each length of embroidery thread and then tie all the ends together with an overhand knot (see diagram A for Rose Pink, page 38).

2 Hook the paperclip through the looped end of all the threads, then place it over a picture hook or something similar (diagram A).

3 Take a pencil and put it through the threads at the knotted end. Now for the tedious bit! Twist the pencil until all the threads are twisted together in a firm rope, which when released slightly tries to twist on itself. Alternatively, use a spinster tool (see page 15). Hook the threads over the hook, turn the handle and the threads twist together as if by magic!

A

INGREDIENTS

- ◎ 5 glass lamp beads, 35–25mm
- ◎ 2 glass lamp beads, 22mm
- ◎ 6 silver-plated bicone beads, 7mm
- ◎ 2 silver-plated large-holed beads, 9mm
- ◎ 14 silver-plated bead caps, 12mm
- ◎ 2 silver-plated square calotte crimps
- ◎ 2 sterling silver crimp beads
- ◎ 2 x 8mm (3/8in) lengths of 'silver' gimp
- ◎ 300mm (12in) length of thick nylon-coated wire
- ◎ 2m (79in) each of 4 different colours of embroidery cotton (floss) to suit your beads
- ◎ 1 large paperclip

4 When the threads are well twisted, put the looped tied ends together, and the threads will automatically twist on each other to form a firm cord.

5 Cut each end of the cord neatly to the desired length and attach one square calotte crimp to each end, following Steps 2–3 of Making a Thong Necklace, page 18. Thread two large-holed beads over the calotte crimps and onto the cord. These will later slide down either side of the necklace to cover the crimps and can be glued in place if required.

6 Attach one end of the nylon-coated wire to the loop of one of the square calotte crimps at one end of the cord using a length of gimp and a crimp bead, following the instructions for Simple Necklace Stringing, page 16. Refer to the photograph to thread on your beads. Attach the other end of the beaded wire to the other square calotte crimp as before.

Hair Bells

- Ease of making: 1
- Time to make: 30 minutes
- Length: 150mm (6in)

Looking just like the delicate harebells of the English countryside, the feature beads of this hair-slide lend themselves perfectly to drop-style jewellery and would look equally good as earrings. Here, I have simply strung them on nylon-coated wire and added them to a heart-shaped slide. As an alternative, the drops could be attached to an elastic hair band or another type of slide.

The large beads are another example of the skilled handiwork of Tuffnell Glass of Yorkshire, England (see page 126) and they are available in other colours. Like all beads from Tuffnell's, the glass used in their production is Venetian and therefore of the highest quality.

INGREDIENTS
- 2 Harebell glass beads, 17 x 15mm
- 2 light amethyst Swarovski crystal bicone beads, 7mm
- 4 light amethyst Swarovski crystal bicone beads, 4mm
- 4 gold-plated beaded rondels
- 5 goldfill crimp beads
- medium mauve AB-coated rocailles
- small pale blue AB-coated rocailles
- 1 'gold' jump ring
- 1 'gold' hair-slide
- 300mm (12in) length of nylon-coated wire
- 250mm (10in) length of nylon-coated wire

Curly Wurlies Earrings

- Ease of making: 3
- Time to make: 15 minutes
- Length: 75mm (3in)

Now for a designer 'bead' with a difference! Is it a bead or is it a pendant? Certainly you can thread through the 'curl', but it also has a loop from which it can be suspended, so it is a bit of both! As soon as I saw these delightful shapes, which are made in many colours by Tuffnell Glass (see page 126), this pair of earrings came to mind, and it was very easy to make them – with, I think, a delightful result.

INGREDIENTS
- 2 Curly Wurlies, 35mm
- 2 Swarovski crystal oval beads, 4 x 7mm
- 2 Swarovski crystal round beads, 4mm
- 2 silver-plated fancy 'figure-of-eight' link bars
- 2 'silver' headpins, 50mm
- 2 'silver' jump rings
- 2 anodized niobium straight-leg angular ear-hooks

A single headpin with a suspended Swarovski oval crystal is hung within the swirl of the bead/pendant, with both the curly pendant/bead and the headpin drop fastened to a 'figure-of-eight' link bar with a single jump ring. So, all you need to do is to refer to the photograph for the design and follow the instructions for Basic Earring Making, page 18, to form loops and make the ear-hooks.

Forget-me-not

— Ease of making: 1
— Time to make: 30 minutes
— Length: 540mm (21¼in)

This necklace shows how just a few special beads can be intermingled with others to produce jewellery of striking style, but without the cost of using only expensive designer beads.

Forget-me-not, the feature bead, displays the soft colours of springtime and called out for other beads of matching delicacy. I found them in the form of old Venetian beads from Jewelex (see page 126), one of my US suppliers. The two long oval beads on either side are also designer beads and like the main one are made by Tuffnell Glass of Yorkshire, England (see page 126); their matt finish is an ideal foil for the sheen of the other glass beads. The look is perfect for spring and summer, and the necklace looks great worn over a simple cream blouse.

The necklace is one of the most simple to make. Refer to the photograph for the threading sequence and follow the instructions for Simple Necklace Stringing, page 16. Turn to page 19 for more advice on the 'filler' beads – if you decide to use these, they should fit inside the hole of the 30 x 23mm glass lamp bead.

INGREDIENTS

- ◎ 1 glass lamp bead, 30 x 23mm
- ◎ 4–5 'filler' beads
- ◎ 2 glass lamp beads, 30 x 14mm
- ◎ 10 glass lamp beads, 12mm
- ◎ 6 glass lamp beads, 10mm
- ◎ 4 glass lamp beads, 10mm, in a different colour
- ◎ 2 silver-plated teardrop beads, 14 x 4mm
- ◎ 24 silver-plated beaded rondels, 5 x 4mm
- ◎ 12 silver-plated cone-shaped bead caps, 8mm
- ◎ 2 silver-plated flower bead caps, 12mm
- ◎ 8 silver-plated bead caps, 8mm
- ◎ 2 sterling silver crimp beads
- ◎ 2 x 8mm (3/8in) lengths of 'silver' gimp
- ◎ 1 silver-plated toggle clasp
- ◎ 600mm (24in) length of nylon-coated wire

Water World

- Ease of making: 8
- Time to make: 4 hours
- Length: 560mm (22in)

While searching for beads on the Internet, I discovered the website of Dora Schubert – and an array of beautiful and expensive one-off beads (see page 126). I have made one of these the focal point of this necklace. Each of Dora's beads is identified by a name and this one, appropriately for the swirling deep water colours incorporated in the glass, is Water World.

Because this is a one-off bead, you will not be able to re-create this necklace exactly, but you can purchase a feature bead of the same size and then use the 'ingredient' list and method below to make a necklace to the same design.

Large handmade beads such as these are very likely to have a big hole, up to 4mm in diameter. If you thread such a bead directly onto relatively thin thread, it will not hang correctly. To overcome this problem, I thread on small beads that fit neatly into the hole of the larger bead and slide out of sight, reducing the size of the hole (see page 19).

INGREDIENTS

- 1 glass lamp bead, 30 x 24mm
- 4–5 'filler' beads, to fit inside the hole of the above bead – see page 19 (not always necessary)
- 2 gold-plated 'coin' washers with a central hole and at least 3 outside holes, 18mm
- 2 gold-plated beads, 8mm
- 6 gold-plated long tube-shaped beads, 14 x 4mm
- 2 gold-plated star-shaped beaded rondels, 7mm
- 16 gold-plated beaded rondels, 5mm
- 2 'gold' beads with a hole large enough to take 4 threads of nylon-coated wire, 5mm
- 2 different colours of rocaille to suit your focal bead
- 6 'gold' square calotte crimps
- 4 'gold' jump rings
- 12 goldfill crimp beads
- 8 inexpensive crimp beads for use as temporary 'stoppers'

- 1 gold-plated toggle clasp
- 4 x 450mm (17¾in) lengths of nylon-coated wire
- 2 x 100mm (4in) lengths of rat-tail or to suit your requirements

1 Take one of the lengths of nylon-coated wire and thread on the large bead. Thread on the smaller 'filler' beads and slide them inside the large bead.

2 On either side of the large bead, thread on a 5mm beaded rondel, an 18mm 'coin' washer and a gold-plated 8mm bead. Centre all these beads in the middle of the wire and use crimp pliers to squeeze a goldfill crimp bead onto the wire either side of the gold-plated 8mm bead to hold all the beads firmly together (diagram A).

3 Thread onto either side of this length of wire a 5mm beaded rondel, 5 small rocailles, a 5mm beaded rondel, 5 small rocailles, a 5mm beaded rondel, followed by about 50 small rocailles. Thread through a goldfill crimp bead and a gold-plated 5mm bead, then thread on about 35 more small rocailles. Apply an inexpensive crimp bead to both ends and secure in place as a temporary 'stopper'.

4 Take each of the other lengths of thread and, following the design from the photograph, choose different but toning rocailles to thread between the coin washers, adjusting the amount to suit the size of your main bead. Thread on a 5mm beaded rondel before threading through a hole in the 'coin', then thread on one more 5mm rondel. When all three wires are threaded, centre the large bead on the wires and secure each in place with a goldfill crimp bead (diagram A).

5 Thread each of the these three wires with the same rocailles as in Step 4, but also, on either side of the main bead, thread one of the long tube-shaped beads onto each wire, being careful that they are staggered in position, i.e. none should be immediately adjacent to another (see photograph opposite and diagram A). Assuming that these rocailles are the same size as those on the first wire, one wire should have about 50 beads and the other two about 56 beads. This will ensure that the necklace hangs correctly.

6 Thread all three wires through the goldfill crimp bead and the gold-plated 5mm bead. Check that all four lengths of threaded wire drape well together. Thread onto each wire about 35 rocailles to match the first length of wire threaded. On completing each one, apply an inexpensive crimp as a temporary 'stopper'.

7 When all threading is finished either side of the large bead, remove the temporary crimps, one at a time, and thread each of the four wires on either side through a goldfill crimp bead (diagram B). Check again to make sure that the necklace drapes well. When you are satisfied, squeeze the crimp bead closed to secure; it is best not to use crimp pliers for this because you need the crimp to remain flat.

8 Trim the excess wire as close to the crimp bead as possible. Cover the wire ends and goldfill crimp bead with a square calotte crimp (diagram B), following Steps 2–3 of Making a Thong Necklace, page 18.

9 Attach a square calotte crimp to either end of each length of rat-tail, as before. Use a jump ring to attach one length to each side of the beaded section (see photograph and diagram B), following Steps 4–5 of Making a Thong Necklace, page 18.

10 Use two more jump rings to attach the finished necklace to the toggle clasp, as before.

Spring Garden

- Ease of making: 5
- Time to make: 2 hours
- Length: 610mm (24in) plus 115mm (4½in) tassel

The large bead, also by Dora Schubert (see page 126), that forms the pendant of this necklace is softly pretty and reminiscent of spring, so I set out to find complementary beads to enhance this look. I think the results are perfect. Once again this is a bead that cannot be replicated exactly, but you should be able to find others that are similar (take a close look at the Flora necklace, page 67) and so be able to make a necklace of the same design.

The delicate focal bead has blue flowers and pale green stems set into, and beneath, crystal clear glass. It gives the impression of pale periwinkles and coiling tendrils floating in water. In a contrast of texture but a match to the green stems, I have made the main necklace with frosted pale green glass beads and the tassel in various shades of pale blue/green to enhance the subtle shades of the flowers. The hole of this bead is not as large as the one in Water World on page 70, so instead of filling it with smaller beads I have simply inverted two 4mm bead caps, which sit inside the hole and hold the bead central on the thread.

A tassel should have free movement, so I chose a very fine thread for the beaded rocailles. The result is very fluid, if somewhat fragile, so you would need to be careful not to snag it on anything.

INGREDIENTS

- ◎ 1 glass lamp bead, 22mm
- ◎ 80 frosted glass beads, 6mm
- ◎ 54 gold-plated bead caps, 4mm
- ◎ 2 gold-plated cone-shaped bead caps, 8mm
- ◎ 1 gold-plated star-shaped beaded rondel, 7mm
- ◎ 3 different colours of rocaille to match your focal bead
- ◎ 1 'gold' headpin, 50mm
- ◎ 2 goldfill crimp beads
- ◎ 1 gold-plated toggle clasp
- ◎ 700mm (27½in) length of nylon-coated wire
- ◎ 9 x 300mm (12in) lengths of fine beading thread (or polyester sewing thread)
- ◎ flexible twisted wire beading needle
- ◎ gel superglue

1 The tassel is made up of nine threads and each colour of rocaille is used three times. Thread the needle with a 300mm (12in) length of thread and thread on three rocailles, leaving enough thread free to tie an overhand knot over the beaded thread (diagram A).

A

2 Pull the knot tight and slide it down to the beads so that they form a triangle (diagram B).

B

3 Using a headpin for application and being very careful not to touch the beads, apply the tiniest possible touch of superglue to the knot. Use a tissue to wipe off excess glue and then cut off the spare thread as close as possible to the knot (diagram C).

C

4 Thread on about 44 more rocailles in one of the other colours. Remove the needle and lay the thread length on a flat surface while you repeat Steps 1–4 eight more times, each time varying the length of threaded rocailles slightly.

5 When all the lengths of rocailles are completed, thread the needle with all the ends of thread at once. Thread through a cone-shaped bead cap, the star-shaped beaded rondel, a 6mm frosted bead, a 4mm bead cap (inverted so that its pointed end sits inside the hole of the focal bead), the focal bead, another inverted 4mm bead cap and a 6mm frosted bead.

6 Pull all the threads so that the top end of each length of threaded rocailles sits inside the cone-shaped bead cap, and then with all threads together, tie an overhand knot as close as possible to the last threaded

6mm bead. Before tightening this knot, make sure that there is just enough slack in the thread for the rocailles to move gracefully but without any thread showing.

7 As in Step 3, apply a small amount of superglue to the knot. Trim the excess thread close to the knot.

8 Form a loop in the 'head' end of the headpin (diagram D), following Steps 3 and 5 of Basic Earring Making, page 18.

9 Thread the headpin through the knotted threads so that the loop catches up the threads; the 'head' of the headpin helps to make sure that the threads do not slide off the loop (diagram E). Tighten the loop around the threads to secure.

D

10 Pass the headpin through the second cone-shaped bead cap. Pull it up tight so that the knotted thread ends are hidden beneath the bead cap.

E

11 Trim the headpin wire to leave about 8mm (⅜in). Form a loop in this length of headpin (diagram F).

12 Referring to the photograph for the design and following the instructions for Simple Necklace Stringing, page 16, make up the necklace, threading on your focal bead and tassel at the halfway point.

F

Ethereal Garden

- Ease of making: 4
- Time to make: 1½ hours
- Length: 470mm (18½in)

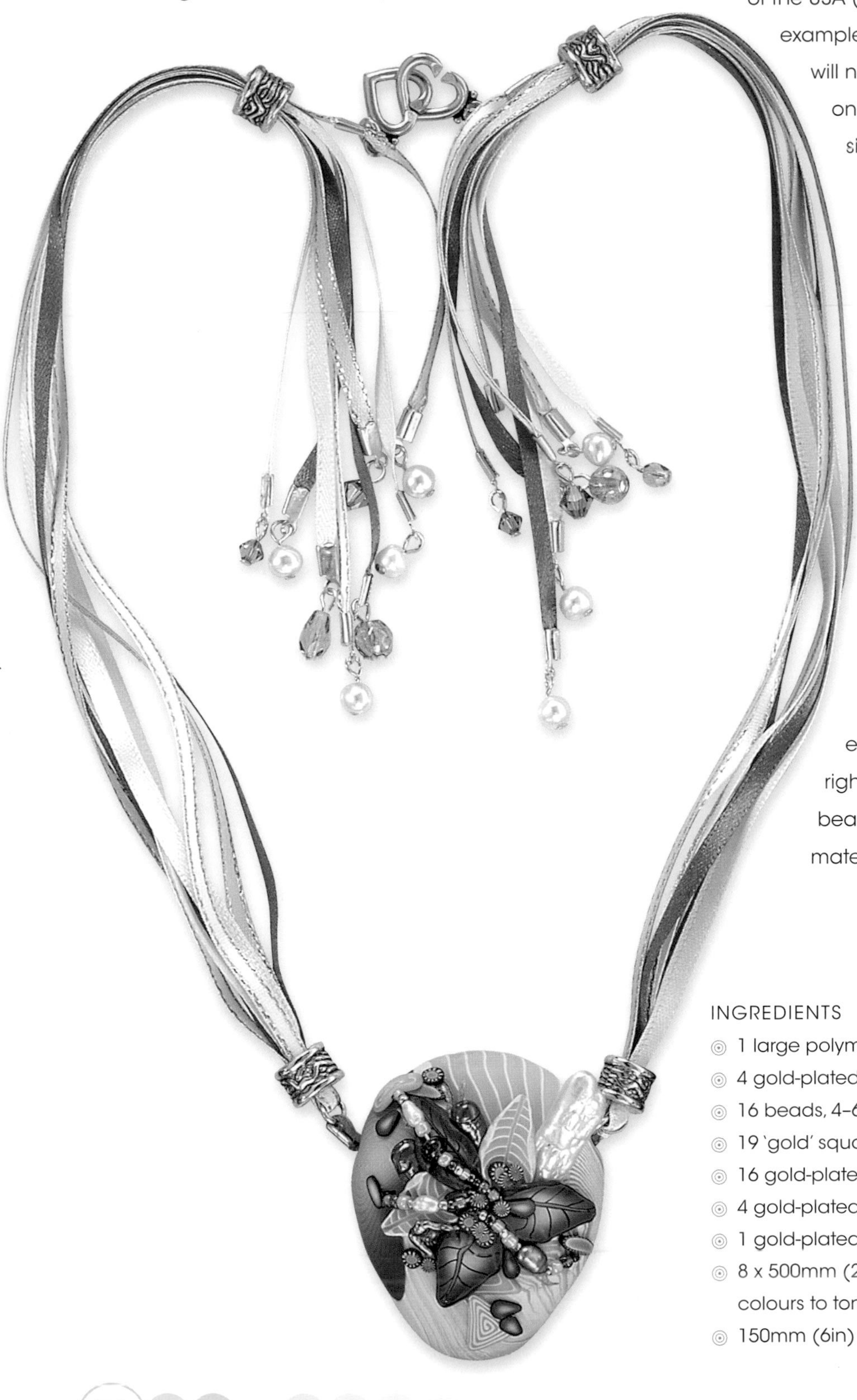

Now for a designer with a difference! The truly fabulous main bead used in this project is from Klew Expressions of the USA (see page 126). Klew's website has other examples of her great beads, so although you will not find a bead exactly the same as this one-off, you will be able to find others of similar quality and style. This bead is made from polymer clay, not glass, and I am so inspired by its complicated beauty that I want to experiment again with that material. In my previous book, *Making Beaded Jewellery*, there are some basic techniques for making your own polymer clay beads, but Klew's beads are real art. Achieving such perfection of detail requires much practice and experimentation!

A bead such as this calls for something very special by way of design, so I set off to my local haberdashery to find these perfectly toning ribbons. Then I sat down to experiment. I think the finished result is just right and lends itself to use with any special bead, be it polymer clay, glass or any other material.

INGREDIENTS

- ⊙ 1 large polymer clay bead
- ⊙ 4 gold-plated large-holed beads, 9mm
- ⊙ 16 beads, 4–6mm, to tone with your focal bead and ribbons
- ⊙ 19 'gold' square calotte crimps
- ⊙ 16 gold-plated headpins
- ⊙ 4 gold-plated jump rings
- ⊙ 1 gold-plated clasp
- ⊙ 8 x 500mm (20in) lengths of 4mm ribbon in 4 different colours to tone with your focal bead
- ⊙ 150mm (6in) length of toning ribbon

1 Take the short length of ribbon and thread on a jump ring to the centre, then thread the two ends through your focal bead. Pull the ribbon ends so that the jump ring is up tight to the bead.

2 Thread another jump ring onto one of the two ends of ribbon. Keeping the threaded ribbon and jump ring as tight to the bead as possible, either stitch the ends together or use a square calotte crimp, with the looped end cut off. Trim the excess ribbon – very little of this ribbon should remain visible (diagram A).

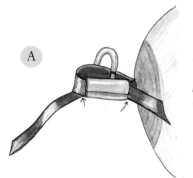

A

Trim excess ribbon at position indicated by arrows

3 Thread 4 different colours of ribbon through one of the jump rings, then thread all the ribbon ends through 2 gold-plated large-holed beads. Slide one bead down the ribbons until it is close to the jump ring.

4 Adjust the ribbons so that they are very roughly equal in length, but allow small differences.

5 Attach a square calotte crimp to each of the ribbon ends, following Steps 2–3 of Making a Thong Necklace, page 18.

6 Adjust the second bead so that the necklace is the correct length for you (see photograph), then thread one of the ribbons so that it loops around, and back through the bead. Check again that the bead is in the right position for your required length of necklace. Apply another square calotte crimp to the ribbon just threaded through the bead, 8–10mm (½in) from the bead (diagram B).

7 Using a jump ring, attach one side of the clasp to the square calotte crimp that you have just fixed in place (diagram B).

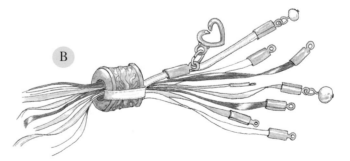

B

8 Apply a bead to each ribbon end using the headpins and following the instructions for Basic Earring Making, page 18.

9 Repeat Steps 3–8 to make the other side and complete the necklace.

Have a Hat?

- Ease of making: 1
- Time to make: 5 minutes
- Length: 150mm (6in)

Distant Landscapes

Petunia

Summertime

It's a Wrap

Violet

Down to Earth

Jungle Green

Celtic Knot

Today, not many women wear hats, and those that do are unlikely to use a hatpin. But these 'beads on pins' remain popular, probably because hatpins are a splendid way to display precious beads. So, here are a few of my special designer beads, with two made up as a more wearable stick-pin. The instructions are general and apply to each of the designs shown, although those ones with the bent-over top are threaded in a different type of sequence.

Violet, Petunia, Summertime and Jungle Green are all made by Tuffnell Glass of Yorkshire, England. Like all their beads, they are available in a selection of other colours or can be specially ordered to suit your requirements. Violet and Summertime are very chunky and ornate. I have gone a little over the top with Summertime by combining it with crystal beads, which, to my mind, gives it the look of a

grand Russian empress. Petunia is a gorgeous bead with a beautiful 3D effect and large petunia-like blooms that almost hide the blue of rosemary flowers beneath their large petals. Jungle Green is very different and, like Dora Schubert's amber-coloured Down to Earth, has intermingling swirls of colour and a glossy finish. The other two thick disc beads are also Dora's. Distant Landscapes is a striking bead with the appearance of a sand picture and Celtic Knot is a translucent bead with a see-through mirror-like surface. Last but not least, It's a Wrap arrived from Klew Expressions of the USA just in time to be included here. It is a beautiful hand-made polymer clay bead and held within its 'ribbon' wraps is a lovely peacock-coloured freshwater pearl.

Refer to page 126 for details of the various suppliers mentioned here.

INGREDIENTS

◎ 1 large bead
◎ several smaller beads to suit the large bead
◎ 1 long twisted metal heishi (tube bead)
◎ 1 hollow metal bead, 3mm
◎ 1 hatpin, 150mm
◎ gel superglue

1 Thread your beads onto the hatpin.

2 For the penultimate bead, choose something with a hole that slips easily over the hatpin. I have used a large heishi. Just at the position where that will sit when slid up to the other beads, apply a very small amount of gel superglue. Do not allow this to touch your special designer bead or anything else that is valuable to you! Slide this penultimate bead up to its final position.

3 Use a hollow 3mm metal bead, or something similar that is a very tight fit to the hatpin, and force it onto the hatpin to slide up to the other beads. To avoid accidents, put the protector onto the pointed end of the pin as soon as the bead is past the tip. Of course, always keep hatpins well out of reach of young children.

4 If making one of the stick-pins, thread the end bead on first and then use general-purpose pliers to gradually bend the wire to form a curve that suits the shape of your main bead. If this first bead is flat, as here, you may also glue it in place to stop it spinning around.

All Alone

— Ease of making: 1–2
— Time to make: 10 minutes
— Length: variable

Very often, designer beads are so striking that to put more than minimal accompaniment with them would be to 'gild the lily'. The gallery over the page shows you several different ways in which a single bead (or pendant) may be suspended from cord, leather or ribbon to show itself off to best advantage.

Because each designer bead requires an individually chosen accompaniment, there are no 'Ingredients' or instructions. Refer to the instructions for Making a Thong Necklace, page 18, which covers all the skills required.

Millie

Like Golden Leaves, this necklace has as its focus a pendant rather than a bead, suspended on 4mm ribbon. The pendant's millefiore decoration owes its origins to the skills of early Venetian bead makers, who developed the technique of producing millefiore cane. This is glass rod that, like a seaside stick of sweet rock, has its floral design running all through its length. To achieve the look seen here, slices of this cane are cut, applied beneath a layer of clear glass and heated in the same way as a glass lamp bead to produce the desired shape and the tactile smooth glossy appearance.

Golden Leaves

If simple is your style, this one is for you! The uncluttered look is easy on the eye and the method is also simplicity itself. This eye-catching pendant and the rich orange-coloured one on page 77 are made by Tuffnell Glass (see page 126). Strictly speaking they are not beads, because instead of a through hole they have a loop from which they are suspended, although bead lovers everywhere are sure to love the gold-leaved appearance of the superior aventurine glass. The latter is glass cane that contains fine copper finings.

Water Iris

Another Tuffnell Glass bead made from Venetian glass – beautiful isn't it? The gorgeous sparkle beneath the crystal clear glass is conferred by a dichroic layer, which nccds careful handling in manufacture to show off its distinctive appearance. On the surface of the bead, near its base, are some gorgeous little raised flowers that remind me of bog irises. Once again the chosen pendant styling and method are simple, with a necklace closure that does not usc a clasp. After the pendant has been threaded onto the thong, tie the ends (not too tightly) in an overhand knot around the other side of the thong. These knots will then slide over the thong to give a necklace of variable length.

Funky Yellow

This fun bead, made by Tuffnell Glass, is available in other colours, slightly different designs and also in a variety of sizes, so there is plenty of choice. Unlike most pendants, Funky Yellow is not threaded on a headpin, but instead onto a Change-a-Bead pendant. This device is a 35mm (1¼in) metal bar with a screw-on bead at the lower end and a bead with a loop, through which to thread cord or whatever at the top. The idea is that you can change beads easily without remaking the whole necklace. In reality, it is rare to find a bead that fits the pendant exactly, but you can solve this by adding a few complementary beads, which just enhances the look.

Purple Heart

This gorgeous baroque heart from Tuffnell Glass is a rich purple colour with gold, decorated with raised roses. The hole of the bead is large, so, before threading the niobium headpin, I put a matching rocaille and a beaded rondel onto the pin. This had to fit, but not slide, inside the main bead. With the headpin inside the large bead, I threaded on smaller beads to fill the space, finishing at the top with a slightly larger bead, which would not completely slide inside the hole. The completed heart pendant was then suspended, by a triangle jump ring, from a large-holed bead that was threaded onto a ribbon of open-weave fabric in mixed metallic colours. The completed effect looks both old-fashioned and modern at the same time, and is sure to appeal to all ages.

Life on Mars

Here we have another bead from Dora Schubert (see page 126). I have left its name unchanged as the almost liquid look to the swirling pattern is reminiscent of something from outer space. It is a fascinating bead to peer into and deserves the best of everything to match its quality. I have chosen simplicity and just a length of plaited cotton cord from which to suspend its heavy teardrop shape. For once, the Change-a-Bead pendant fitted the bead exactly, so there was no need to add any extra beads. The fastener is a variation of the trigger clasp, in the shape of a playful dolphin – who knows, perhaps once dolphins lived on Mars!

ORIENTAL TREASURES

T he Chinese really are masters in the art of enamelling and all fine bead work, and the projects here show two different aspects of the Chinese bead-makers' craft. Intricate enamel bead work can usually be attributed to these meticulous craftsmen, and these three projects showcase different examples of these beautiful beads. Recently they have also made huge strides in their glass bead making and now lamp beads from China rival the best of the rest. However, the glass beads used for the Birds of Paradise earrings, page 82, display an old skill that is described in the project introduction. Many traditional Chinese beads depict folklore and I am sure that these glass beads are no exception. I only wish I knew the significance of the birds and also that I could read Chinese in order to understand the writing on the blue enamel beads!

The earrings that follow range from simple to relatively time consuming to make. However, none are difficult, so you should simply refer to the photograph for the design and follow the instructions for Basic Earring Making, page 18.

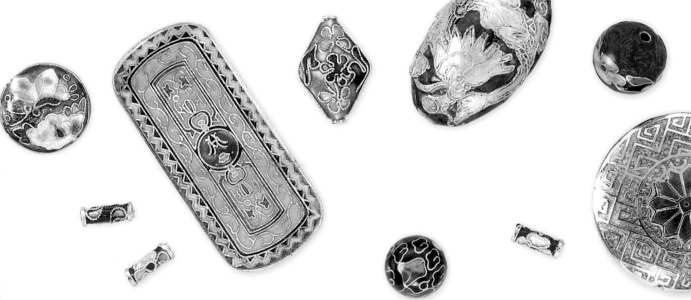

Imperial Blue

- Ease of making: 5
- Time to make: 2 hours
- Length: 520mm (20½in) plus 70mm (2¾in) drop

The colour and style of these beads is so rich and regal that only the best in supporting beads would do. I therefore chose high-quality Bohemian lamp beads, beautiful blue bugles and niobium jewellery wire to complete the 'picture'. The lamp beads are from Europe and have a clear glossy surface with underlying goldstone that 'breaks up' to reveal a central core of blue, which almost exactly matches the blue of the enamel beads. Even the screw clasp is chosen to match and in use it looks somewhat similar to the 10mm lamp beads.

All the beads and the niobium wire used here are available in other colours, offering a variety of options for you to choose from. Remember when using pliers (with the exception of cutting pliers) to manipulate niobium wires to cover the jaws with clear adhesive tape to protect the anodized surface.

INGREDIENTS

- ◎ 3 'pillow' enamel beads, 45mm
- ◎ 6 blue/gold glass lamp beads, 10mm
- ◎ 3 blue/gold tube-shaped glass lamp beads, 20 x 8mm
- ◎ medium 'gold' rocailles
- ◎ small matt-finish blue rocailles
- ◎ 17 matt-finish blue bugles, 10mm
- ◎ 12 'gold'-lined bugles, 7mm
- ◎ 2 gold-plated rosebud drops
- ◎ 16 'gold' anodized niobium jump rings
- ◎ 2 blue anodized niobium jump rings
- ◎ 2 'gold' square calotte crimps
- ◎ 1 gold-plated round screw clasp, 9mm
- ◎ about 1m (39in) blue 22-gauge anodized niobium wire
- ◎ about 120cm (47in) 'gold' 22-gauge anodized niobium wire

1 Cut two 100mm (4in) lengths of blue niobium wire and one 100mm (4in) length of 'gold' niobium wire. Place all the wires in a square calotte crimp and use general-purpose or flat-nosed pliers, applying firm pressure, to secure the calotte crimp closed over the wires. Refer to the photograph to thread the three wires with rocailles and bugles.

2 Place one of the jump rings over the three wires (diagram A), then make a loop in the end of each wire, following Steps 3 and 5 of Basic Earring Making, page 18. Open a 'gold' niobium jump ring and loop it through all three loops just made in the niobium wire.

A

3 Thread all the beads (with the exception of the central 'pillow' bead) with appropriate lengths of blue niobium wire and make loops at either end, following the instructions for making connectors in Step 1 of Golden Wedding, page 65. Each 'pillow' bead has a definite hole for threading through two of the opposing corners, but because these beads are made from two pieces of metal 'welded' together, the other corners usually also have holes, which will enable the wire threading shown in diagram B. However, be sure to retain a bead with at least three good corner holes for the central bead.

4 Cut an 80mm (3¼in) length of blue niobium wire and make a loop in one end as before, curve the wire and thread it so that the end appears from the bottom hole (not the opposing one) of the bead. Leave about 8mm (⅜in) of wire straight and then form a loop

(diagram B). Repeat from the other side of the bead, but use a slightly shorter length of niobium wire.

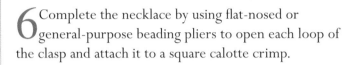

5 Referring to the photograph for the design, assemble the necklace using 'gold' niobium jump rings to connect all the wired beads together.

6 Complete the necklace by using flat-nosed or general-purpose beading pliers to open each loop of the clasp and attach it to a square calotte crimp.

Birds of Paradise

└ Ease of making: 3
├ Time to make: 15 minutes
└ Length: 55mm (2¼in)

If these large glass beads were made of solid glass, they would be too heavy to use for earrings, but in fact they are made from blown glass and therefore only half the weight that you might expect. The decoration is also not what it might seem, as the perfectly hand-painted birds are not on the outside of the glass but inside. This method of decoration was demonstrated to me on a visit to a small shop in Singapore's Chinatown. The artist uses very fine paintbrushes, some of which comprise only a single hair, that are angled at the 'head' end in order to reach otherwise inaccessible areas of glass. The decoration on all beads of this type is flawless – not an easy task when applied to the outside, but just consider trying to achieve this perfection when painting through a small hole on the inside of the glass!

I have not noted the colour of any beads in the 'ingredients' list, as the main bead is available in various colours and decorative options, so you may wish to choose a different scheme.

INGREDIENTS
◎ 2 hollow glass beads, 18mm
◎ 2 crackle glass beads, 8mm
◎ 4 silver-plated beaded rondels, 4 x 6mm
◎ 2 silver-plated bead caps, 4mm
◎ 4 'silver' oval beads, 2 x 4mm
◎ 2 small rocailles
◎ 2 sterling silver headpins, 50mm
◎ 2 sterling silver straight-leg angular ear-hooks

Empress Drops

Ease of making: 3
Time to make: 45 minutes
Length: 85mm (3¼in)

These earrings are made in a similar style to the Rainbow Fluorite Chandeliers in Earring Fest, page 121, but are very different in appearance, showing just what a change of bead can do for a design. The main beads are Chinese handmade cloisonné and I feel they give a rather noble look, hence the name!

INGREDIENTS

◎ 8 Chinese cloisonné tubes, 10 x 4mm
◎ 26 gold-plated faceted bicone beads, 4mm
◎ 2 small gold-plated drops
◎ 2 goldfill beads, 2mm
◎ 2 medium red rocailles
◎ 12 'gold' headpins, 50mm
◎ 2 gold-plated 3–1 necklace ends
◎ 2 goldfill straight-leg angular ear-hooks

These earrings are made in a similar way to the Imperial Blue necklace, page 81, in that the drops are formed by making a series of connectors from headpins.

Through the Hoop

Ease of making: 4
Time to make: 30 minutes
Length: 85mm (3¼in)

Large earrings such as these should not be heavy, otherwise they drag badly on the earlobes, so here I have used hollow lightweight Chinese enamel as the feature beads. They are beautifully made and available in about five other colours and several different designs. I have made the hoop, on which they are strung, from a length of bracelet-length memory wire, which is not easy to bend and form into a loop, but it is worth the trouble because it also confers strength on the earring, making it almost impossible for it to become misshapen.

INGREDIENTS

◎ 2 Chinese cloisonné beads, 16mm
◎ 54 Czech crystal faceted bicone beads, 3mm
◎ 14 beaded rondels, 4mm
◎ 4 silver-plated bead caps, 4mm
◎ 2 sterling silver faceted beads, 2mm
◎ 2 anodized niobium headpins, 50mm
◎ 2 'silver' jump rings
◎ 2 anodized niobium straight-leg angular ear-hooks
◎ 2 lengths of small bracelet-size memory wire

GOING FOR A THONG

This time we have a section centred around a type of necklace rather than a type of bead, because at almost any point in the evolution of fashion you will find beads or pendants threaded in this way. Take a look, for instance, at Victorian chokers, and often you will see a simple cameo threaded on velvet ribbon, then survey the range of contemporary jewellery and you are sure to come across plenty of examples of threading on thong, ribbon or cord. I will also show you different ways to use the same bead, since beading really is all about using your imagination and, as you will discover, the beads themselves can often lead the way.

Disco Choker

- Ease of making: 1
- Time to make: 15 minutes
- Length: 500mm (20in)

The first project is a simple but very effective necklace for casual wear. The large discs are inexpensive Indian lamp beads, and those used in between are made from gold-plated pewter with a large hole. The thong is a soft suede. Together, these few 'ingredients' make a striking necklace. The disc beads are available in six colours, but as they are handmade, the colours and sizes may not be the same for each bead, so you will need to choose carefully to find beads that are a fairly close match.

INGREDIENTS

- ◎ 5 deep mauve glass disc beads, 24mm
- ◎ 6 gold-plated large-holed beads, 8mm
- ◎ 2 gold-plated square calotte crimps
- ◎ 1 'gold' hook clasp
- ◎ 2 x 600mm (24in) lengths of suede in contrasting colours

1 Place one end of the two lengths of suede together inside the open calotte crimp (diagram A), then secure the crimp onto the thong, following Step 3 of Making a Thong Necklace, page 18.

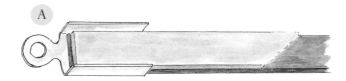

A

2 Cut the other two ends of the suede to a diagonal point to enable easy threading (diagram B).

B

3 Thread both lengths of suede through one of the large-holed metal beads and slide this bead along until you have it positioned at about 150mm (6in) from the calotte. If you want your necklace to be longer or shorter than the one shown here, you will need to adjust this position.

4 Thread both lengths of suede through one glass disc bead from opposite sides (diagram C). Slide the glass disc bead up to the metal bead.

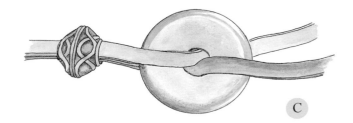

C

5 Thread both lengths of suede through another large-holed metal bead. Slide this metal bead up to the glass disc bead, so that it appears as in the photograph.

6 Continue following Steps 4—5 until all the beads are used, ending with a metal bead.

7 Cut the two ends of the suede square and to match the length of the other side of the necklace, then repeat Step 1 to secure the ends in the other square calotte crimp.

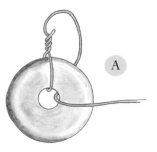

8 Use flat-nosed or general-purpose pliers to open the loop of the hook clasp sideways and attach it to one of the calotte crimps (diagram D).

Starry Night Choker

- Ease of making: 6
- Time to make: 45 minutes
- Length: 450mm (17¾in) plus 70mm (2¾in) drop

To demonstrate very different ways of using beads, I set about creating a contrasting necklace to the Disco Choker, featuring the same large disc beads but in an alternative guise. I stumbled across this design while wiring a single bead for a small choker, and it occurred to me that others could be added to make a larger pendant. Then, having wired the beads together, there still seemed to be something lacking, but after a few false starts, I found the perfect solution – 3mm Swarovski bicone beads, which became the stars in an inky sky! I have worn this necklace several times and on each occasion it has given rise to compliments and queries about where to obtain something similar. So, without further ado, take your pick of the bead colours and the many different-coloured jewellery wires available and get beading!

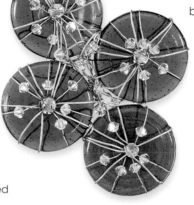

INGREDIENTS

- 4 deep mauve glass disc beads, 24mm
- 29 clear AB-coated Swarovski crystal bicone beads, 3mm
- 4 clear AB-coated Swarovski crystal faceted round beads, 4mm
- 2 'silver' square calotte crimps
- 1 'silver' hook clasp
- 1m (39in) length of fine jewellery wire
- 500mm (20in) length of rat-tail

1 Thread one end of the 1m (39in) length of jewellery wire through one glass disc bead and then wind the wire around the bead, as shown in diagram A. Twist the wires together to secure, as shown.

2 Continue to thread the wire though the central hole, and from inside to outside, around the first bead. After a few times, wire on the other three beads, as shown in diagram B, pulling the wire as taut as possible. At first, the added-on disc beads will not seem at all secure or be firmly in position, but as you progress they will become a solid unit.

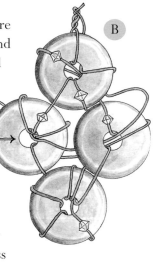

B

3 While threading the wire in and around the beads, add the 3mm crystal bicone beads to the front of one side of the 'pendant', finishing with a 4mm crystal faceted round bead threaded into the centre of each disc bead, to disguise the wires that disappear into the holes.

4 When you are satisfied with the appearance and firmness of your pendant, bring the end of the wire back up to the top, where you started, and wind the wire from the central hole around the bead in loose loops, from inside to outside and from bottom to top, several times. Wind the wire sideways around the base of the loops at the top of the disc bead, incorporating the original lengths of twisted wire, to form a loop from which to suspend the 'pendant' (diagram C).

5 Make up the thong from which to suspend the pendant using the rat-tail, square calotte crimps and hook clasp, following the instructions for Making a Thong Necklace, page 18.

C

Bead on a Chain

— Ease of making: 3
— Time to make: 10 minutes
— Length: 460mm (18in)

This is one of the simplest projects in the book, although I give it a difficulty rating of 3 because some people have trouble with making loops in wire, required to suspend the bead on a headpin. It is yet another version of the thong necklace and once more it shows how good a special single bead can look as a pendant. This bead is from Tuffnell Glass of Yorkshire, England (see page 126), and the chain is sterling silver in a style known as 'snake'.

INGREDIENTS

◎ 1 focal bead (this one is 30 x 17mm)
◎ 2 bead caps, 4mm
◎ 2 rocailles in a colour to suit your focal bead
◎ 1 x 460mm (18in) ready-made sterling silver chain
◎ 1 sterling silver headpin, 50mm

No method is given, as the only skills needed to make this item are those for bending the headpin wire into a loop, for which the instructions are given in Basic Earring Making, page 18.

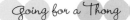

SENSATIONAL SHELL

Shells have been used for jewellery for at least 75,000 years (see page 6), and today we still carry on the same tradition. Tourist shops the world over sell simple drilled shells as jewellery, and nearly everyone must have picked up a special shell from the beach and wondered what to do with it. Some shells are truly spectacular and exhibit a wonderful lustred rainbow of colours, and it is these most appealing items that are usually used for beads. The coloured side of shells is always on the inside and therefore not easily displayed. Also, many shells, such as the abalone, are large and consequently have limited uses in jewellery as whole specimens. However, modern techniques have provided us with the means to utilize this unique natural material and beautiful beads made from shells are available to us all.

Abalone Drops

└ Ease of making: 6
└ Time to make: 1½ hours
└ Length: 460mm (18in) plus 27mm (1in) drop

Of all shells, perhaps the abalone (or paua) is the most renowned for colour, with waves of blues and greens reflecting its marine origin. In an attempt to improve on nature, abalone shell is often dyed, but the results are frequently bright and garish blues, reds and purples that owe little to nature. The colour of the abalone used in this necklace is as the shellfish made it, and simply cut and polished to enhance the watery hues.

INGREDIENTS

◎ 1 tapered set of abalone shell
◎ 42 matt-finish emerald glass beads, 4mm
◎ 26 oily-finish blue faceted bugles, 2mm
◎ 52 gold-plated bead caps, 4mm
◎ 2 'gold' calottes
◎ 1 'gold' round clasp, 10mm
◎ 710mm (28in) length of blue/green beading thread
◎ bottle of liquid superglue or a flexible twisted wire beading needle

1 Follow Step 7 of Black Magic, page 41, to stiffen the first 50mm (2in) of the thread using the bottle of superglue, or you can use a flexible twisted wire beading needle if you prefer.

2 Tie a substantial knot in the end of the beading thread, then carefully apply a very small touch of superglue to the knot. Wipe off the excess with a tissue and use sharp scissors to trim the excess thread. Pass the thread through the hole of one calotte so that the knot is concealed inside the 'shell' of the calotte. Use flat-nosed or general-purpose beading pliers to close the calotte.

3 Thread on a 2mm faceted bugle, a bead cap and a 4mm bead, then tie a knot following Step 3 of Modern Tradition, page 57. Thread on another 4mm bead and tie another knot. Refer to the photograph for the remaining threading sequence, tying knots between

each of the 4mm beads, until you have threaded seven sequences of 4mm beads.

4 Thread on the tapered set of abalone shell, spaced with bugles and bead caps, as shown in the photograph. Complete the other side of the necklace to match the first and then finish by using your pliers to open the loops of the calottes, attach the clasp and then close them.

Seashore Keepsake

└ Ease of making: 3
└ Time to make: 30 minutes

INGREDIENTS

◎ 1 small abalone (paua) shell (or similar with natural holes through the shell)
◎ 10 small freshwater pearls
◎ 1 abalone cabochon, 10 x 8mm
◎ 10 fine headpins, with as small a head as possible, 50mm
◎ 1 bar brooch back, 25mm
◎ gel superglue or epoxy glue

How many times have you walked along a beach and found a beautiful shell? At least once I am sure, and then when you returned home with your treasure in your pocket, what did you do with it? My bet is that somewhere it still lingers in a jar or junk box. Well, here is an idea for one type of shell. I found this one on a beach in Crete, but it is fairly common, so keep your eyes to the ground when walking that sandy cove. My idea was to create a brooch that imitated a rather prolific oyster, which held within its shell not one but a whole clutch of pearls!

The method of making this brooch is simple, as these shells have naturally occurring holes through which the headpins can be threaded.

1 Thread one pearl onto a headpin and then find a hole in the shell and thread the headpin through, threading from the inside of the shell towards the outside of the shell.

2 Trim the spare headpin wire to leave about 8mm (⅜in), then use flat-nosed or general-purpose pliers to bend this short length down onto the shell, making sure that it is secure, holds the pearl firmly in place and that the ends are as tight to the shell as possible (diagram A).

A

3 Repeat Steps 1–2 until all the pearls and each hole is used or until you are satisfied with the effect.

4 Use the superglue or epoxy glue sparingly and carefully to glue the abalone cabochon in place.

5 Apply the superglue or epoxy glue over the bent headpin wire ends at the back of the brooch to help secure them and also to seal in any sharp ends.

6 Use superglue or epoxy glue to stick the brooch bar to the back of the shell – you may need to bend this slightly so that it fits the curve of the shell. Place out of the reach of small children to allow the glue to dry.

Bunny Bangle

⌐ Ease of making: 2
├ Time to make: 10 minutes
└ Length: 170mm (6¾in) (expandable)

INGREDIENTS

◉ 2 through-drilled shell rabbits, 35 x 20mm
◉ 26 'silver' oval beads, 7 x 5mm
◉ 2 'silver' beads, 2mm
◉ 1 bracelet length of memory wire

Beads come in many shapes other than round, but these little rabbits must rate as some of the most unusual. Originating from Asia, they are made from large black mother-of-pearl shell and are thick enough to have a hole drilled through from top to bottom. The overall effect is brown on one side and white on the other, with a nacre iridescence that catches the light in bands of rainbow colour. A child of any age is sure to be captivated by a gift of jewellery that incorporates one or two of these enchanting little beasts! Here, they are threaded onto a length of memory wire, together with 'silver' beads, to create a charming bangle.

1 Use strong general-purpose pliers to bend over about 3mm (⅛in) of one end of the length of memory wire. Continue bending until the wire is completely bent back on itself towards the inside of the circle of wire (diagram A). This wire is strong and

(A)

very resistant to bending, so this does take a little force and care is required so that the wire does not hurt you. It is therefore definitely not a task for children!

2 Refer to the photograph to thread on the beads, then repeat Step 1 to complete the bracelet.

Shades of the Sea

—Ease of making: 4
—Time to make: 2 hours
—Length: 470mm (18½in)

INGREDIENTS

◎ 400mm (15¾in) length of 13mm square abalone beads (this is enough for both the necklace and bracelet)
◎ 7 silver-plated flower links
◎ 2 teal anodized niobium jump rings, 4mm
◎ 1 silver-plated clasp
◎ 600mm (24in) length of teal anodized niobium wire

Like Abalone Drops, page 89, both this necklace and the almost matching bracelet are made from natural-coloured abalone shell. However, these beads do owe some of their qualities to man! They are a similar colour and texture on both sides and in nature this would be impossible, so these beads have an acrylic filling (like the jam in a sandwich) and the surface too has a light acrylic coating to give a smoother and more glossy effect than would otherwise be possible. But the gorgeous wave-like swathes of iridescent marine hues are the product of nature alone.

To match the colours of the beads, I have used teal-coloured niobium wire as the threading medium and the beads are simply linked together with this strong and colourful material. The bracelet is made in exactly the same way as the necklace and to make both you simply need to refer to the photograph for the design and follow Step 1 of Golden Wedding, page 65, to make beaded connectors with the niobium wire.

WILD ABOUT WIRE

Wire is a threading and beading medium that really does set the imagination free with seemingly unlimited colours and types of wire available. There are many examples of wire use throughout this book, for example the Imperial Blue and Shades of the Sea necklaces and bracelet, pages 81 and 91, which were made using niobium wire, and the Bunny Bangle, page 90, and the Rainbow Choker, page 46, where memory wire formed the basis of the projects. However, here, as in Starry Night Choker, page 86, I use a more traditional beading wire, which is available in various thicknesses and many colours – see page 13.

Captive Heart

- Ease of making: 6
- Time to make: 1 hour
- Length: 360–460mm (14¼–18in)

This delicate-looking necklace has a rose quartz heart as its main feature and is threaded on a necklace length of memory wire. It could even be worn as a bridal choker, yet despite its fine, elegant appearance it is a robust necklace that will never break. It is not too difficult to make, although you may need to experiment a few times before you are satisfied with the wiring of the central stone.

The shape of the main bead is especially appropriate for rose quartz, as when this stone is carved into a heart shape, it is reputed to attract love! So guys, if you are reading this, perhaps you should take note and look out for a rose quartz heart as a gift for the lady in your life!

INGREDIENTS

◎ 1 rose quartz heart, off-centre-side drilled
◎ 6 matt-finish 'gold' beads, 5mm
◎ 14 matt-finish 'gold' beads, 3mm
◎ 2 'gold' open-wire beads, 7mm
◎ 2 'gold' fancy washer beads, 5mm
◎ 2 'gold' metal or glass bugles, 10mm
◎ 4 'gold' glass crystal bicone beads, 4mm
◎ 140 medium white pearl rocailles
◎ 1¼ coils of necklace-length memory wire
◎ 500mm (20in) length of 'gold' wire

1 Bend one end of the memory wire, following Step 1 of Bunny Bangle, page 91, and then refer to the photograph above to thread on the beads. When threading is completed, finish off the memory wire by bending it as before.

2 Wind the 'gold' wire tightly around one end of the memory wire, tucking the end out of sight. Wind in a spiral along the length of the necklace. When you reach the heart bead, wind the wire around it following Step 2 of Entrapped Carnelian opposite, then continue spiral winding to the end. Wind the wire around the end of the memory wire, trim and tuck the end out of sight.

Entrapped Carnelian

- Ease of making: 6
- Time to make: 4 hours
- Length: 440mm (17¼in)

INGREDIENTS

- ◎ 12 flat carnelian beads, 30 x 5mm thick
- ◎ 12 sliver-plated headpins, 50mm
- ◎ 2 silver-plated flower links for use as necklace ends
- ◎ 1 hook clasp
- ◎ 3m (3¼yd) length of 'silver' fine wire

1 Thread each carnelian bead with a headpin and make a loop at either end, following Step 1 of Golden Wedding, page 65, for making connectors.

2 Open one of the headpin loops just made and attach it to one end of a flower link, then cut a 250mm (10in) length of wire, push one end of this wire inside the hole of the bead next to the flower link and wind the wire around the headpin wire to secure. Then wind the wire around the bead, and sometimes beneath and around the wound wire, pulling the wire taut as you go (diagram A). When you are happy with the appearance of your 'parcelled' bead and all the wire is tight against the bead, finish as at the beginning of this step by winding around the other end of the headpin wire and tucking the end of the jewellery wire out of sight inside the hole of the bead.

3 Open another of the headpin loops made earlier and attach it to the loop of the wired

Carnelian and silver look good together, and as soon as I saw these carnelian beads, this design sprang to mind. The beads themselves are beautiful, and being flat they are translucent and so show off the 'graining' in the stone better than round beads. This means that even simply strung they would look stunning, but wire-wrapping each one gives another textural dimension and adds visual interest. The beads themselves were made in China, although the stone originated in Brazil.

bead (diagram A). Repeat Step 2 to wire this bead and continue in this way until all the beads are wired and connected together. However, prior to wiring the last bead, attach it to the other flower link.

4 Complete the necklace by attaching the hook clasp to the other ends of the flower links.

A

BIRTHDAY BEADS

Probably everyone has heard of birthstones and knows a little of their meanings, even if it is only for the stone appropriate to their own month of birth or astrological sign. But there is much folklore, legend, myth and mystery attached to all the natural 'stones', and for each month/astrological sign there is a choice of several 'stones' that could be considered appropriate. So, to give you plenty of scope for choice, here is a list of the signs of the zodiac, with four of their corresponding 'stones'.

Capricorn	December 22nd–January 20th	garnet, hematite, onyx, malachite
Aquarius	January 21st–February 19th	amethyst, aquamarine, pearl, hematite
Pisces	February 20th–March 20th	jasper, bloodstone, aquamarine, coral
Aries	March 21st–April 19th	diamond, sapphire, garnet, rock crystal
Taurus	April 20th–May 20th	emerald, jade, lapis lazuli, chrysotile
Gemini	May 21st–June 20th	agate, aventurine, turquoise, pearl
Cancer	June 21st–July 22nd	ruby, moonstone, sapphire, turquoise
Leo	July 23rd–August 22nd	amber, carnelian, diamond, topaz
Virgo	August 23rd–September 22nd	agate, aventurine, chrysocolla, peridot
Libra	September 23rd–October 23rd	citrine, opal, chrysoprase, lapis lazuli
Scorpio	October 24th–November 21st	topaz, pearl, alexandrite, labradorite
Sagittarius	November 22nd–December 21st	lapis lazuli, ruby, turquoise, bloodstone

Autumn Sunshine

- Ease of making: 6
- Time to make: 1 hour
- Length: 470mm (18½in)

Citrine is a type of quartz with a clear golden colour of varying depth and shade that seems most appropriate for October, or Scorpio, which in the northern hemisphere is an autumnal month. It is reputed to prevent nightmares, ensure sound sleep and to protect from bad happenings, although of course you may choose to wear it or give it as a present just because it is beautiful!

The appeal of this necklace lies in its elegant simplicity and, being knotted, it drapes well. Once you have mastered the skills of knotting, as shown in the Modern Tradition pearl necklace, page 57, it is easy to make. The diamond-shaped, gold-plated open beads are just large enough to hold a 4mm Swarovski crystal with a small rocaille at either side, and these little insertions add interest and sparkle to the finished necklace. Citrine beads such as these are frequently sold as ready-made jewellery items and are inexpensive to purchase, but once knotted and re-strung, they have a look and feel of quality. The clasp is magnetic and strong enough to keep closed during wear, but easy to undo when required.

INGREDIENTS

- 1 necklace length of 10 x 7mm flat oval citrine beads
- 5 gold-plated open diamond-shaped beads
- 5 topaz-coloured Swarovski crystal bicone beads, 4mm
- 10 'gold' rocailles
- 2 x 8mm (³/8in) lengths of 'gold' gimp
- 1 gold-plated magnetic clasp
- 500mm (20in) length of coloured beading thread
- gel superglue

1 Attach the length of thread to the clasp, then thread on 12 citrine beads and make knots in between each one, following Steps 1–4 of Modern Tradition, pages 57–58.

2 Thread through a hole of one open diamond-shaped bead, then thread on one rocaille, one Swarovski crystal bicone and one more rocaille. Pass the thread out through the opposite hole in the open diamond-shaped bead (diagram A).

3 Refer to the photograph for the remaining threading sequence and complete the necklace using the techniques in Steps 1–2.

A

Winter Blues

— Ease of making: 1
— Time to make: 20 minutes
— Length: 480mm (19in)

We all link winter with the colour blue, so, perhaps appropriately, the rich royal blue lapis lazuli is associated with the winter month of December. It is remarkable that such a strong colour could be naturally occurring, although lapis lazuli is often colour-enhanced to improve stones of lesser quality. However, the colour of the beads used in this necklace is natural and the stone is from Afghanistan, where it has been mined for more than 6,000 years. It is often believed that lapis lazuli occurs with gold flakes in the stone, but these are actually iron pyrites, and you can see examples of this within some of the beads shown here.

For thousands of years, lapis lazuli has been prized by man. The Pharaohs of ancient Egypt treasured it as a heavenly colour of the afterlife and painted their tomb ceilings with the ground stone. Today we still prize it, mostly for its colour, but also for its magical powers, since it is reputed to confer protection and peace, promote gentleness, healing and soothing and even to ensure fidelity between lovers!

INGREDIENTS

◎ 400mm (15¾in) necklace length of lapis lazuli, average bead size 20 x 15mm
◎ 12 gold-plated bead caps, 10mm
◎ 4 gold-plated beaded rondels, 4 x 6mm
◎ 8 medium blue rocailles
◎ 1 large gold-plated toggle clasp
◎ 500mm (20in) length of nylon-coated wire

To make up the necklace, refer to the photograph for the threading sequence and follow the instructions for Simple Necklace Stringing, page 16.

Amazing Amethyst

- Ease of making: 8
- Time to make: 5 hours
- Length: 520mm (20½in) plus 130mm (5in) tassel

Amethyst is one of the most spectacular of semi-precious stones and, like citrine, is a member of the quartz family. It appears in a gorgeous array of pale milky mauve to deep clear purple colours, which were conferred by tiny amounts of iron impurities present during its formation millions of years ago. It is believed that amethyst promotes happiness, love, healing, peace, courage, intelligence and justice, so, as a simple good-luck stone or a birthstone for the month of February or Aquarius, you couldn't choose better!

The majority of the beads in this necklace are simply amethyst coloured, but the largest focal beads are the real thing, and their baroque style is perfect for the random method of stringing the other beads. Like citrine, amethyst is easily available and often found as ready-made jewellery at very reasonable prices; the beads used here were taken from an inexpensive elasticated bracelet.

Beginners to bead jewellery making might take one look at this necklace and turn the page, but it really is quite easy to make. All you need is a little patience and time!

INGREDIENTS

- 6 baroque amethyst beads, 17 x 10mm
- 25 peacock-coloured freshwater pearls, 8mm
- 9 amethyst-coloured faceted glass teardrops, 10 x 7mm
- 4 amethyst-coloured faceted glass teardrops, 7 x 5mm
- 22 amethyst-coloured faceted glass beads, 4mm
- 20 amethyst-coloured faceted glass beads, 3mm
- 80 amethyst-coloured glass beads, 4mm
- 250 mixed rocailles in various shades of amethyst
- 20 clear AB-coated glass bugles
- 10 mixed 'silver' heishi (tube beads)
- 10 mixed fancy amethyst coloured glass beads, 6–8mm
- 50 mixed 'silver' beads, 3–8mm
- 2 bicone beads, 7mm
- 1 large-holed 'silver' bead, 25 x 20mm
- 1 amethyst-coloured crystal heart
- 16 'silver' crimp beads
- 1 silver-plated toggle clasp
- 8 x 450mm (17¾in) lengths of nylon-coated wire

1 Before beginning to thread, check that each of the baroque amethyst beads that are intended to take multiple threads can accommodate the number required and if necessary either enlarge holes with a bead reamer (see page 15) or choose different beads.

2 Attach four lengths of nylon-coated wire onto each part of the toggle clasp using 'silver' crimp beads without gimp and following the instructions for Simple Necklace Stringing, page 16.

3 Begin threading one side of the necklace by passing all four wires through one 6–7 mm amethyst bead and then continue to thread beads onto each length of wire (for this first section, choose fairly small beads and bugles). When each wire has about 40mm (1½in) of threaded beads, thread all four through one 6–8mm 'silver' bead.

4 Once again threading each length of wire separately, thread on another random sequence of beads. This time mingle larger beads with the smaller ones, but avoid positioning them close to the point where all threads pass through a larger bead. When each wire has about 50mm (2in) of threaded beads, thread all four through one of the baroque amethyst beads.

5 Repeat Step 4 twice more and then thread all four wires through a 7mm bicone bead and then through the large 'silver' bead.

6 Repeat Steps 3–5 with the four lengths of wire on the other side of the necklace. You should now have eight lengths of wire emerging from the lower end of the large silver bead. Referring to the photograph on page 97 for the threading sequence, thread each of these with beads. Finish each length of wire with a different bead and at a slightly different length from each other. Use flat-nosed or general-purpose pliers to apply a crimp bead to the end of each wire. Use cutting pliers to remove any excess wire and your lucky amethyst necklace is complete!

The World is Spinning

- Ease of making: 1
- Time to make: 10 minutes
- Length: 540mm (21¼in)

So, now that you have read all about the other semi-precious stones, perhaps you can't make up your mind which one is for you? Well, this little easy project could help! Just look closely and you can see that the bead of this pendant is a world in miniature. The sea is made from reconstituted lapis lazuli and the continents from a variety of different semi-precious stones. Each bead is handmade and slightly different from any other, and they are a delight to either wear yourself or to give as a gift.

INGREDIENTS
- 1 globe bead, 22mm
- 1 gold-plated flat bead, 8mm
- 1 gold-plated small necklace end
- 1 'gold' headpin, 50mm
- 2 'gold' square calotte crimps
- 1 'gold' hook clasp
- 600mm (24in) length of suede thong

Make up the pendant using the headpin and following the instructions for Basic Earring Making, page 18, then follow the instructions for Making a Thong Necklace, page 18, to complete the necklace.

Lucky Jade

- Ease of making: 3
- Time to make: 15 minutes
- Length: variable

People the world over believe in jade as a bringer of fortune. For centuries, New Zealand Maoris handed heirloom pieces from father to son, considering the stone to have powers over the weather, while in Mexico the Mayans believed that jade would bestow harmony, peace and accord on both the environment and the populace. Such was the acceptance by the Chinese that jade was a lucky stone that even the poorest would carry a piece with them, believing that its virtue would be absorbed into the body. Even in present times, jade is worn in China to denote a person of high standing and office.

It is often assumed that all jade is green and that it is all the same type of stone. It is true that the bright green variety is the most treasured and widely recognized jade, but its many colours include white, yellow, orange, purple, dull blue, grey or brown. But these huge variations are due, in part, to the fact that several varieties of stone fall under the term jade, most commonly nephrite and jadeite, but also Chinese soo chow jade, a soft, pale translucent green, and the 'Australian jade', chrysoprase. The elephant in this necklace is carved from pure jade, but the other stones used are soo chow and nephrite.

INGREDIENTS

- 1 jade elephant
- 1 silver-plated bead cap, to form the elephant's saddle
- 11 nephrite beads, 8mm
- 8 soo chow beads, 7–10mm
- 17 soo chow beads, 4–6mm
- 9 green Swarovski crystal bicone beads, 3–4 mm
- 4 green Swarovski crystal bicone beads, 7mm
- a few rocailles in small, medium and/or large sizes in 3 different but toning greens
- 2 'silver' square calotte crimps
- 1 silver-plated toggle clasp
- 3 x 1m (39in) lengths of fine jewellery wire in 'silver', green and black

Although this necklace looks complicated, it is quite simple to make and is in fact just a three-strand version of Wired Gold, page 111, so follow those instructions to make up the necklace and refer to the photograph for the threading sequence. To achieve the effect seen here, the necklace should be lightly twisted after making to entwine the wires slightly. However, it looks equally good if the wires are left untwisted.

BEADED GEMS

In addition to birthstones (see page 94), there are many other examples of beautiful natural stones available that should not be missed, so in this section I focus on a few of these special gems. There is something about beads made from the fabric of our earth that gives them a unique appeal. Maybe it is the fact that the material is older than time or because each bead is subtly different from every other one, or perhaps their charm lies in the mystery, legends and beliefs that are associated with each one.

Mother of the Bride

- Ease of making: 6
- Time to make: 3 hours
- Length: 400mm (15¾in)

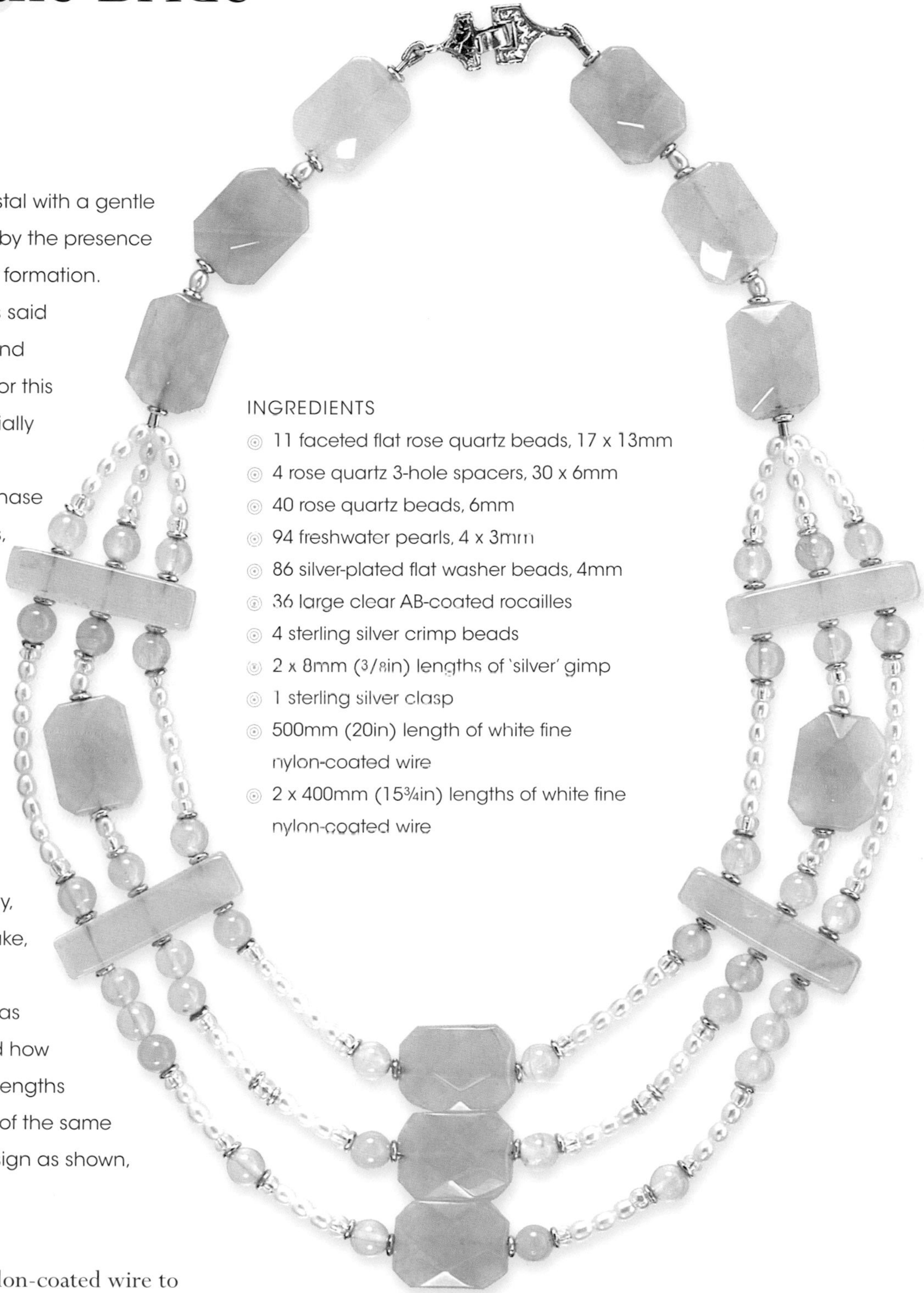

Rose quartz is a decorative rock crystal with a gentle rose pink colour that was conferred by the presence of titanium or manganese during its formation. A popular stone of feminine hue, it is said to promote love, friendship, peace and happiness, which makes its choice for this Mother of the Bride necklace especially appropriate.

Rose quartz is inexpensive to purchase and comes in a wide range of forms, from simple round beads and shapes, such as those seen here, to carved pendants. The three-hole spacer bars and round beads were taken from a ready-made bracelet, which can be found in gift shops or bead catalogues, and the faceted beads were taken from a loose-strung 400mm (15¾in) length.

Like so much handcrafted jewellery, this necklace appears difficult to make, but once again it is quite easy. The challenge lay in the design, which has to allow for different-sized beads and how they affect the spacing of the three lengths of beads. So, if you purchase beads of the same sizes as these and just follow the design as shown, you should have no problems.

INGREDIENTS

- ◎ 11 faceted flat rose quartz beads, 17 x 13mm
- ◎ 4 rose quartz 3-hole spacers, 30 x 6mm
- ◎ 40 rose quartz beads, 6mm
- ◎ 94 freshwater pearls, 4 x 3mm
- ◎ 86 silver-plated flat washer beads, 4mm
- ◎ 36 large clear AB-coated rocailles
- ◎ 4 sterling silver crimp beads
- ◎ 2 x 8mm (3/8in) lengths of 'silver' gimp
- ◎ 1 sterling silver clasp
- ◎ 500mm (20in) length of white fine nylon-coated wire
- ◎ 2 x 400mm (15¾in) lengths of white fine nylon-coated wire

1 Attach the longest length of nylon-coated wire to the loop of one part of the clasp using the gimp and a crimp bead, and following the instructions for Simple Necklace Stringing, page 16. Refer to the photograph for the threading sequence to thread on the beads. After threading the third faceted rose quartz bead, thread on one crimp bead.

2 Thread the first 10mm (½in) of the two 400mm (15¾in) lengths of nylon-coated wire through the crimp and the washer beads and into the faceted rose quartz bead (make sure that the ends stay out of sight inside the hole of this bead). Ensuring that there is no slack in the beaded section of wire, use crimp or general-purpose pliers to squeeze the crimp bead down onto the wires – see diagram A for Indian Ocean Blues, page 33.

3 Refer to the photograph on page 101 for the threading sequence to thread beads onto each wire. When you reach the same point as at the beginning of Step 2, thread on a crimp bead and, after adjusting the wires to ensure that there is only enough slack for the necklace to hang correctly, apply the crimp bead as before.

4 Trim the two shorter lengths of wire to leave only about 10mm (½in) and then, making sure that these two ends are inside the hole of the first faceted rose quartz bead, continue threading. Finish off the necklace as at the beginning of Step 1.

Matching Earrings

└ Ease of making: 3
├ Time to make: 15 minutes
└ Length: 50mm (2in)

Because the holes in the pearls used in these earrings are so small, I have been unable to use headpins on which to suspend the beads and have instead threaded the beads on fine nylon-coated wire. You will find the instructions for using this for earrings in Midnight Pearl Earrings, page 61.

INGREDIENTS

◎ 2 faceted flat rose quartz beads, 17 x 13mm
◎ 2 freshwater pearls, 4 x 3mm
◎ 2 large clear AB-coated rocailles
◎ 6 silver-plated flat washer beads, 4mm
◎ 4 sterling silver crimp beads
◎ 2 sterling silver ear-hooks
◎ 2 x 30mm (1¼in) lengths of nylon-coated wire

Tantalizing Tourmaline

— Ease of making: 3
— Time to make: 30 minutes
— Length: 500mm (20in) plus 50mm (2in) drop

If you are familiar with the usual pink/green/mauve versions of tourmaline, you may well not recognize the beads seen here as the same stone and it is certainly less frequently seen. These crystals, which have here been roughly fashioned into beads, are a translucent brown, but the range of colour exhibited by tourmaline is greater than any other stone, so you should not be surprised to find it in many guises!

Although beads such as these may be uncommon, a little searching should be fruitful. But even if you don't find beads exactly the same as these, this necklace style can be used for any large graduated beads and gives a completely new look to an old and perhaps rather uninspiring necklace.

Tourmaline has an unusual property in that when heated or rubbed it becomes electrically charged at one end and will then attract dust and dirt, so if this necklace looks dirty, it is not just because we have the builders in!

INGREDIENTS

⊙ 1 x 400mm (15¾in) length of graduated brown tourmaline crystals
⊙ 6 gold-plated bead caps, 10mm
⊙ 1 gold-plated bead cap, 12mm
⊙ 1 gold-plated cone-shaped bead cap, 10 x 8mm
⊙ 1 gold-plated bail
⊙ 1 'gold' headpin, 75mm
⊙ 2 'gold' calottes, 6mm
⊙ 1 'gold' barrel screw clasp
⊙ 80mm (3¼in) length of 1mm diameter black waxed cotton cord

1 Tie an overhand knot tightly in one end of the length of cotton cord and trim any excess cord close to the knot.

2 Place the knot inside a calotte (diagram A) – note that this is a larger and slightly different type of calotte to those used elsewhere. Use general-purpose pliers to close the calotte.

A

3 Thread on the tourmaline beads, starting with the smallest, and tying a simple overhand knot between each (no need to use the special knot, e.g. as in Modern Tradition, page 57, as this would make too large a knot for the beads and cord). Refer to the photograph on page 103 for the threading sequence and continue threading and knotting the tourmaline beads and bead caps,

remembering to thread on the bail in the centre front of the necklace. Keep the largest bead to make the drop.

4 Repeat Step 1 and then use flat-nosed or general-purpose pliers to open each loop of the clasp and attach it to the loop in each calotte.

5 Thread the 12mm bead cap, the one remaining large bead and the cone-shaped bead cap onto the headpin. Then form a loop in the headpin, following Steps 3–5 of Basic Earring Making, page 18, and attach the drop to the bail at the centre of the necklace.

Chunks of Rock

— Ease of making: 1
— Time to make: 15 minutes
— Length: variable

Chunky drilled semi-precious stone is widely available and perfect for making inexpensive gifts with meaning.

So far male jewellery wearers have been rather neglected, so to redress the balance, the dark necklace is designed to have masculine appeal. The stone is haematine, a reconstructed version of a heavy natural stone called haematite, and as a birthstone for September/Virgo it is reputed to have healing attributes. The cord is 2mm waxed cotton and the smaller beads are wooden. The green necklace features agate, a highly varied stone type with exotic names such as crazy lace and ocean spray. As a birthstone for June/Gemini, it is reputed to confer protection, healing and longevity.

To make the dark necklace, follow the instructions for Making a Thong Necklace, page 18, and tie a simple overhand knot between each bead. To achieve the looped effect of the agate necklace, the thong – a stretchy 'gold' elastic – is threaded through the hole in the stone twice and the loop held in place by using a short length of fine wire to twist around the thong where it crosses, at a point that will be hidden in the bead hole. Otherwise, follow the instructions for Making a Thong Necklace, page 18.

Beautiful Blue Lace

— Ease of making: 4
— Time to make: 45 minutes
— Length: 460mm (18in)

All agate stones are attractive, with a stunning display of parallel bands of colour that, in shape, follow the contours of the cavity within which they were formed millennia ago. Most appear in translucent strong earthy colours, but the beautiful blue lace agate is a special example, with delicate banding and shades of baby blue through to white. It is less commonly seen than most agates, but is still easily available from most bead suppliers.

As with all semi-precious stones, blue lace agate is believed to confer benefits on the wearer and for this stone the attributes are an ability to relieve stress and prevent quarrels, as well as promoting peace and happiness. The darker blue beads in this necklace were an inexpensive purchase from a stall of Chinese artefacts in London's Portobello Road and I believe that they are a dyed chalcedony, another natural stone.

INGREDIENTS

- 15 faceted flat oval blue lace agate beads, 18 x 14mm
- 6 blue-dyed natural stone beads, 12mm
- 4 blue-dyed natural stone beads, 10mm
- 16 imitation opal beads, 6mm
- 3 blue Swarovski crystal bicone beads, 6mm
- 3 blue Swarovski crystal bicone beads, 4mm
- 25 silver-plated flat washer beads, 4mm
- 18 silver-plated beaded rondels, 4mm
- 2 sterling silver fancy cone-shaped end caps, 20 x 12mm
- 2 silver-plated faceted bicone beads, 4mm
- 10 sterling silver beads, 2mm
- 5 'silver' headpins, 50mm
- 2 sterling silver crimp beads
- 1 sterling silver clasp
- 500mm (20in) length of nylon-coated wire

To create this necklace, first make the drops, using the headpins and following the instructions for Basic Earring Making, page 18. Refer to the photograph for the threading sequence, including the positioning of the drops, and follow the instructions for Simple Necklace Stringing, page 16.

MARVELLOUS METALS

Probably because of its malleability, pure silver was one of the earliest metals to be used by humans and we have long associated it with good luck, which is possibly the reason why it is the traditional christening or wedding gift. Together with gold, it is one of the two most frequently used precious metals, and in jewellery making is universally popular, with shops worldwide selling a huge range of all types of necklaces, earrings, bracelets and brooches. So, the challenge here was to provide you with project items that you might not find elsewhere. I hope I have succeeded!

Gold is a beautiful metal, but it is expensive and therefore, in its solid form, infrequently used in beading, so here we have a few alternatives. Throughout the book I have tried where possible to use products that are at least plated with real gold, as this gives the best and most durable finish. However, here, as in some instances elsewhere, this is not always practical and some beads and findings are merely gold-coloured.

Ode to a Wild Rose

—Ease of making: 4
—Time to make: 30 minutes
—Length: 190mm (7½in)

Most silver bracelets are either bangles or chain, so here as an alternative is one made from beads that are in fact not solid silver but very high-quality silver-plated pewter – a material that gives a solid, heavy feel and is of a durable nature. Each of the long beads is beautifully decorated with tiny wild roses in raised profile and the 3mm round beads are sterling silver. The end links, the 2-hole spacers and the clasp are made from the same material as the long beads.

When making a bracelet, it is important to be sure that the clasp is easy to fasten, as unlike a necklace, the wearer only ever has one hand free to do this. With that in mind, the clasp I have chosen is simple and secure.

INGREDIENTS

◎ 16 silver-plated tube-shaped beads, 14 x 4mm
◎ 24 sterling silver beads, 3mm
◎ 3 silver-plated 2-hole spacers
◎ 2 silver-plated 2–1 necklace/bracelet ends
◎ 2 sterling silver jump rings
◎ 4 sterling silver crimp beads
◎ 4 x 8mm (³/8in) lengths of gimp
◎ 1 silver-plated toggle clasp
◎ 2 x 200mm (8in) lengths of nylon-coated wire

To make up the bracelet, refer to the photograph for the threading sequence and follow the instructions for Pearl Cuff Bracelet, page 58.

Silver Drops

—Ease of making: 4
—Time to make: 45 minutes

Beaded brooches are not often seen, but perhaps should be more widely available as they offer a very imaginative way to use beads. Here, as in the Golden Rain Brooch, page 36, I have used a 150mm hatpin as the base on which to build an unusual brooch, which has 'icicles' of silver drops hanging from a bead-threaded bar. Bead lovers should note the particularly charming little 'I Love Beads' pendant.

INGREDIENTS

- 13 silver-plated faceted bicone beads, 5mm
- 25 silver-plated faceted bicone beads, 3mm
- 13 silver-plated beaded rondels, 5mm
- 12 small silver-plated pendants or beads
- 'silver'-lined rocailles
- 1 'silver' hatpin, 150mm
- 24 'silver' crimp beads
- 500mm (20in) length of nylon-coated wire

1 Bend the hatpin to form a brooch base, following Steps 1–4 of Golden Rain Brooch, page 36.

2 Make up the drops using varying lengths of nylon-coated wire with either a bead or pendant at the end of each, following the instructions for Midnight Pearl Earrings, page 61.

3 Refer to the photograph for the threading sequence to thread the beads and drops onto the hatpin.

Butterfly Anklet

└ Ease of making: 1
└ Time to make: 30 minutes
└ Length: 220mm (8½in)

This anklet could also be made as a bracelet, but it would look great for summertime wear with sun-bronzed legs and it is also an item not often seen in the shops. This time most of the materials that I have used are sterling silver, although the butterfly is silver-plated pewter. This little pendant is beautifully made and just one of a big range of drops manufactured by one of my favourite suppliers in the USA, Tierracast (see page 126). However, if you prefer to use an alternative adornment for your anklet, you will find a huge choice in the pages of a good bead catalogue.

I have made this anklet for someone with slimmer ankles than mine, so be sure to measure the ankle for whom the item is intended and if necessary adjust the length. As an item of jewellery to be worn on the ankle, it will be fairly vulnerable, so I have used a safety clasp that cannot accidentally be undone.

INGREDIENTS

- 60 sterling silver faceted beads, 3mm
- 4 links of 4mm diameter sterling silver belcher chain (or use linked jump rings)
- 1 silver-plated pendant
- 2 x 8mm (3/8in) lengths of gimp
- 2 sterling silver crimp beads
- 1 sterling silver clasp
- 250mm (10in) length of nylon-coated wire

To make up the anklet, refer to the photograph for the threading sequence, remembering to thread the pendant chain as you thread the beads, and follow the instructions for Simple Necklace Stringing, page 16. The pendant is added to the chain when stringing is finished and applied by either opening a link of the chain or by using a jump ring.

Silvery Hair-slide

Ease of making: 5
Time to make: 1 hour

Hair ornamentation is easy to source, but finding something unusual can be more difficult, so why not make your own? This hair-slide project is made from an assortment of many types of 'silver' bead, but you could use the same technique to produce a hair-slide that is exactly tailored to your requirements. The slide base itself is also variable and you will be able to choose from the slightly curved shape (as seen) or one that accommodates tied-back hair; the former is also available in up to four lengths.

The metal base on which this hair-slide is made is the same as you will see in many ready-made items, and when you consider the complicated appearance of the back of one of these, you may well wonder how it is possible to successfully create your own hair-slide. But don't worry – these slides are easily taken apart and the section to which the beads are then applied is quite plain.

INGREDIENTS

◎ about 80 'silver' beads in a mix of rocailles, bugles and metal beads
◎ about 600mm (24in) length of 'silver' fine jewellery wire
◎ 1 hair-slide, 80mm

1 Take the hair-slide apart into three pieces as shown, noting the order in which they fit together. The top solid bar with a hole in one end is the only beaded part — put the other two sections, which form the 'clasp', aside.

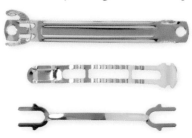

2 Thread the length of wire through the hole of the metal bar and, twisting the wire, securely attach it to the hair-slide (diagram A).

3 Thread onto the wire a length of randomly selected beads to match the length of your hair-slide and lay these along the length of the metal bar, then thread the wire around the other end of the bar and up through the hole at this end. Repeat this twice more so that you have three lengths of threaded beads lying along the length of the bar (diagram B).

4 Now thread two, three or four beads onto the wire and wrap the wire and beads diagonally around the bar over the beads already threaded (diagram B). Keep threading and wrapping the wire in this way, keeping the wire as taut as possible at all times.

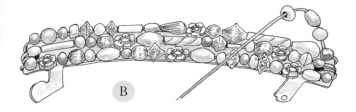

5 When there is no metal bar left visible and you are satisfied with the appearance of your hair-slide, finish off by winding the wire around one of the holes several times and then tucking the end of the wire out of sight beneath the beads.

6 Take the two parts of the 'clasp' that you set aside in step one, reassemble the hair-slide and it is ready to wear!

Great Pretender

- Ease of making: 2
- Time to make: 30 minutes
- Length: 210mm (8¼in)

This bracelet both looks and feels as if it is made from solid gold components. It has a chunky form that is conferred by the main beads, which are actually beaded star-shaped rondels. These are normally used as spacers between other beads, but here, to give an unusual effect, I have threaded them all together. The gold beads and clasp are excellent-quality 22ct gold-plated pewter, with a long-lasting finish and a heavy feel. To add a little sparkle of interest, I have placed, and threaded through, a 6mm Swarovski crystal in the centre of each diamond-shaped bead. I have chosen a bright cerise colour for these, but you may prefer something different or even choose to make the bracelet from silver beads to give an alternative look.

INGREDIENTS

- 76 gold-plated flat star-shaped rondels, 7mm
- 2 gold-plated beaded rondels, 4mm
- 5 gold-plated open diamond-shaped beads, 14 x 12mm
- 5 cerise Swarovski bicone beads, 6mm
- 2 goldfill crimp beads
- 2 x 8mm (³/8in) lengths of 'gold' gimp
- 1 gold-plated Art Deco-style toggle clasp
- 250mm (10in) length of nylon-coated wire

To make up the bracelet, refer to the photograph for the threading sequence and follow the instructions for Simple Necklace Stringing, page 16. The only variation is the threading of the Swarovski crystals within the open diamond-shaped beads, for which you should follow Step 2 of Autumn Sunshine, page 95. However, the crystals used here are a little larger and vary very slightly in size, so for each diamond-shaped bead, it may be necessary to try one or two crystals before you find one to fit properly.

Wired Gold

- Ease of making: 3
- Time to make: 1 hour
- Length: 420mm (16½in)

Wired Gold makes no pretence at being
anything other than a fashion necklace and it is
made from a wide selection of beads, some of which
owe little but their colour to gold. Others are gold-plated
pewter, and the wire and clasp simply have a 'gold' finish.
This is a versatile style of necklace, lending itself well to
making in other colours of both bead and wire. It is also
possible to use the same technique but create another
look by combining several different yet toning
beaded wires to make a multi-strand necklace.

INGREDIENTS

- ⊚ 26 'gold' beads, 6–10mm
- ⊚ 2 gold plated square calotte crimps
- ⊚ 1 'gold' round barrel clasp, 10mm
- ⊚ 1m (39in) length of 'gold' jewellery wire

1 Use flat-nosed or general-purpose pliers to bend
over 4mm (⅛in) at one end of the length of wire.
Apply a square calotte crimp to the end of the wire,
being sure to cover the cut end, following Steps 2–3 of
Making a Thong Necklace, page 18 (diagram A).

2 Thread one bead onto the wire until it is about
30mm (1in) from the calotte crimp. Hold this bead
between your thumb and forefinger and the two strands
of the wire either side of the bead in the fingers of your
other hand. Twist the wire
below the bead three or
four times until it is on a
'stalk' of twisted wire
(diagram B).

A

3 Repeat Step 2 until all the beads are used up. If you
wish to use more beads, in greater density, you
should decrease the space between each one.
Conversely, to use fewer beads, the distance between
each bead should be increased.

4 When you have finished wiring the beads, complete
the necklace by repeating Step 1 and attaching each
part of the clasp to the loop of a calotte crimp.

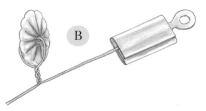

B

ARABIAN NIGHTS

For anyone who loves beads, travel to the Arab countries of North Africa and the Middle East can provide very exciting hunting grounds, as most of these parts of the world have very strong bead-making traditions and old and new beads are to be found in abundance. In fact, even the non-beader is sure to be tempted by the exotic displays of colourful beads often in unexpected places. A few years ago when I was on a felucca sailing boat on the Nile, the 'Captain's' assistant produced a sack of about a hundred locally made, intricate rocaille necklaces for sale, one of which is shown here. I proceeded, much to his surprise and delight, to buy the lot! Most necklaces you see will be new, but lurking in back-street shops and dusty bowls there are almost certain to be some older treasures. So, take a look at these projects to see just a small selection of what you might find in Arab souks and bazaars.

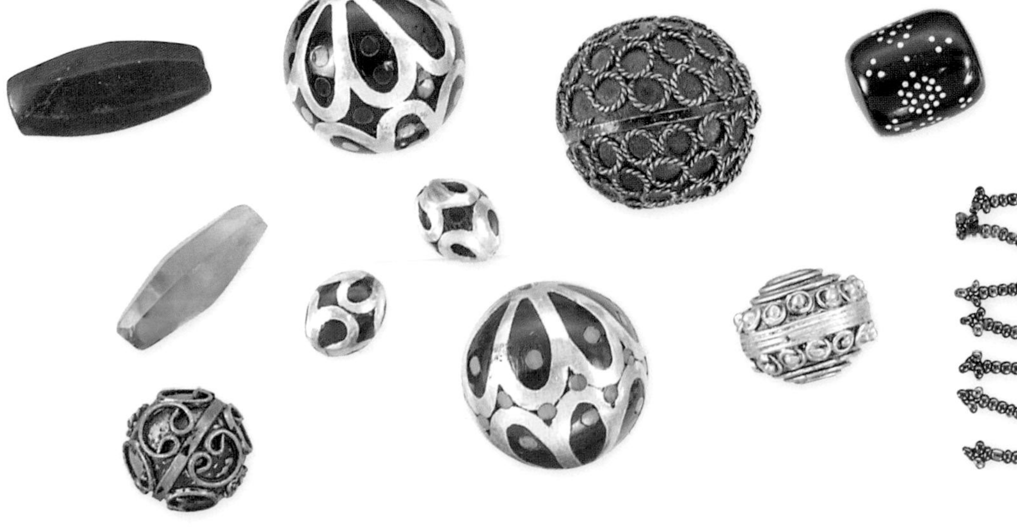

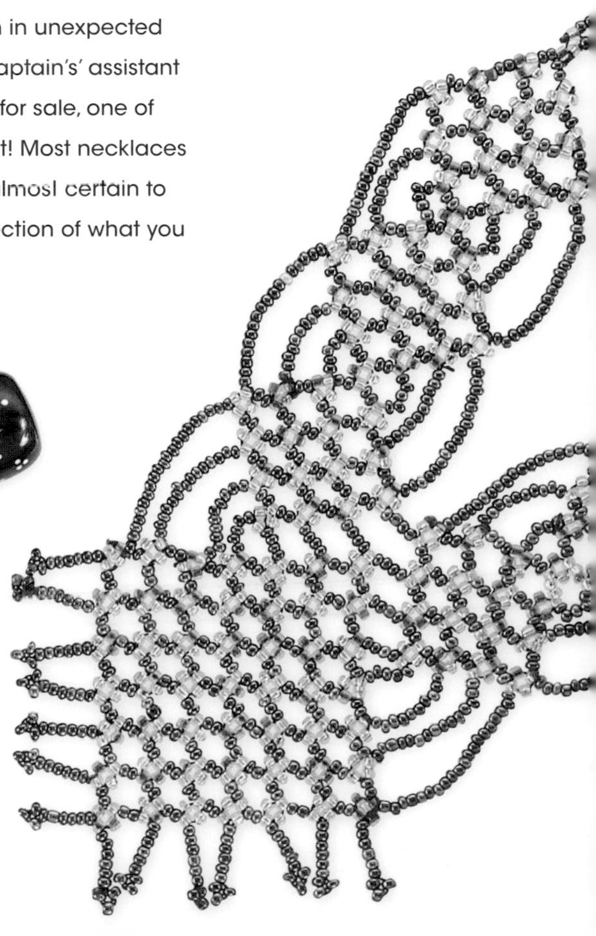

Souk Treasure

Souk Treasure

─ Ease of making: 1
─ Time to make: 30 minutes
─ Length: 450mm (17¾in)

Any bead lover who has visited the fabled city of Marrakech is sure to have been drawn to the souks by the abundance of beaded jewellery to be found there, and I am no exception. On one bead-buying trip, my party stumbled across a grubby shop, where, behind a cobweb-bedecked window, lay a selection of interesting beads. With a gleam in his eye, the vendor pulled the dish of beads from the window and negotiations began. Declining to agree to his high price of 950 Dirhams (approximately £60/$107) for a hen's egg-sized Berber bead, we made a move to leave, but seeing a sale in danger of vanishing, he produced another cache of beads. After much rummaging and bartering, the requested price for our selection was beaten down to just below half and with both parties satisfied we left with our purchases, some of which you can see here. A little farther on, another shop and more beads beckoned. We entered and to our delight found a wonderful mix of both old and new. The handmade metal beads in the

following project came from this second stop on our Moroccan expedition, and you should be able to obtain similar beads today, either from a souk in Marrakech or, rather more easily, from a good bead supplier! To give a lift to the dull appearance of the metal beads, I have combined them with the sparkle of Czech crystal, which is available in a huge range of colours to suit your chosen look.

In an interesting twist to the tale, about 12 months after the Marrakech trip I was wandering around an antiques fair looking for old beads when suddenly I saw a necklace with a hen's egg-sized metal Berber bead as its feature bead, just like the one I saw in Morocco, with a £12 ($21) price tag. The stall owner noticed my interest and, in an attempt to secure the sale said, 'You can have that for £10 ($18)'. Deal done, I handed over the money and reflected on the strange quirks of fate!

To make up the necklace, refer to the photograph for the threading sequence and follow the instructions for Simple Necklace Stringing, page 16.

INGREDIENTS

◎ 1 Moroccan 'silver' bead, 25 x 23mm
◎ 2 Moroccan 'silver' beads, 20 x 8mm
◎ 6 Moroccan 'silver' beads, 12 x 10mm
◎ 30 'silver' bicone beads, 6mm
◎ 10 Czech crystal teardrop beads, 12 x 9mm
◎ 2 'silver' crimp beads
◎ 1 'silver' barrel screw clasp
◎ 500mm (20in) length of nylon-coated wire

Aswan Ancients

- Ease of making: 1
- Time to make: 30 minutes
- Length: 710mm (28in)

To show you more of the wonderful types of bead that you can find while holidaying in exotic locations, I have included this necklace, the beads for which were found in an Egyptian bazaar. All the large beads are old and some, I suspect, may be very ancient and have been in use for many hundreds of years, especially the natural green stone, the white agate ovals and the faceted carnelian – if only they could talk! All the smaller beads are new, but were chosen because they look antique and so suit the style of the necklace.

If you are seeking out beads such as these, you will need to be persistent and search through the artefacts contained in the jars and dishes of street stalls, bazaars and shops. I found these while strolling through the bazaar of the southern Egyptian city of Aswan, where they lurked beneath a pile of broken pocket watches!

In many countries you should also be prepared to negotiate, and when appropriate, I usually start with an offer of a third of the asking price and eventually settle on about half price. Sometimes these negotiations, especially for larger quantities, can be protracted and involve several cups of tea, so be prepared!

Only 13 of the beads used in this necklace are old and not readily available from bead suppliers. But with a little diligent searching, you should be able to find something similar, either on your travels or perhaps in an antique shop or market.

To make up the necklace, refer to the photograph for the threading sequence, stringing your beads in a similar style, and follow the techniques for Simple Necklace Stringing, page 16.

INGREDIENTS

- 13 old beads – mine are as follows:
    - 1 roughly faceted old stone bead, 20 mm
    - 2 white agate beads, 40 x 18 mm
    - 4 faceted carnelian beads, 14mm
    - 2 faceted oval carnelian beads, 25 x 10mm
    - 2 silver ornate oval beads, 20 x 15mm
    - 2 silver barrel beads, 30 x 15mm
- 6 aventurine beads, 8mm
- 4 aventurine beads, 6mm
- 6 white agate beads, 8mm
- 6 carnelian beads, 8mm
- 2 carnelian beads, 6mm
- 14 wooden discs, 8mm
- 2 'silver' flat round beads, 10mm
- 20 'silver' beads, 7mm
- 2 'silver' tube-shaped beads, 8 x 4mm
- 2 'silver' crimp beads
- 2 x 8mm (3/8in) lengths of 'silver' gimp
- 1 toggle clasp
- 800mm (31½in) length of nylon-coated wire

CHARMED I'M SURE

For thousands of years man has associated charms with good luck. For example, the ancient Egyptians carried or wore amulets – charm-like semi-precious stones – in the belief that they would protect them from ill fortune. Today, the traditional charm bracelet is made from a precious metal with a selection of matching pendants suspended from it, but we don't need to stick with tradition when modern materials give us so much greater scope. So, in this section I have looked at different ways of using charms to produce jewellery with a modern edge that is sure to appeal to all ages.

Charming Sparkler

Ease of making: 4
Time to make: 1 hour
Length: 200mm (8in)

This pretty bracelet appears, at first glance, to be of the traditional gold chain variety; that is, until its almost hidden sparkle shines through! The 'chain' on which the bracelet is based is actually linked channel-set Swarovski crystal, which, by itself, is delightful as a jewellery item. It is available from bead suppliers in various lengths and size, shape and colour of crystal, and to use it on its own it is only necessary to adjust it to the required length and add a clasp. However, to give extra interest, I have added many gold-plated pewter charms that have been chosen to match the high quality of the 'chain'.

INGREDIENTS

- 195mm (7¾in) length of channel-set Swarovski crystal 'chain'
- 20 gold-plated charms
- 22 gold-plated jump rings
- 1 toggle clasp

1 Attach a jump ring to each of the charms, following Steps 4–5 of Making a Thong Necklace, page 18, but before closing each jump ring, attach two onto each link of the 'chain' between the coloured crystals.

2 Again using jump rings, attach the clasp to the bracelet and it is completed. Simple isn't it?

Necklace Charms

- Ease of making: 4
- Time to make: 30 minutes
- Length: 440mm (17½in)

Using the same type of 'ingredients' as Charming Sparkler, page 115, this necklace is simpler in appearance and much less expensive to make because it incorporates fewer of the charms and a shorter length of 'chain', although you may, of course, choose to use more of both. The method of adding charms is the same as for the bracelet, but I have used a different method of attaching the suede thong than has been shown elsewhere and that method is detailed below.

INGREDIENTS

◎ 100mm (4in) length of channel-set Swarovski crystal 'chain'
◎ 5 gold-plated charms/pendants in graduated lengths
◎ 8 'gold' jump rings, 5mm
◎ 9 'gold' jump rings, 4mm
◎ 1 'gold' barrel screw clasp
◎ 1 headpin, 50mm
◎ 2 x 180mm (7in) lengths of suede
◎ gel superglue

1 Attach a 4mm jump ring to each of the charms, following Steps 4–5 of Making a Thong Necklace, page 18, but before closing each jump ring, attach one onto each link of the 'chain' between the coloured Swarovski crystals. Attach a 4mm jump ring to either end of the 'chain'.

2 Trim the ends of both lengths of suede at a diagonal and onto one length thread two 5mm jump rings, then thread 10mm (½in) of one end through one of the jump rings at the end of the crystal 'chain'. Using a headpin for application, apply a tiny touch of gel superglue to the threaded end of suede and, being careful not to get the superglue on your fingers, fold the 10mm (½in) length of suede back on itself to secure the jump ring in place. Now simply slide the jump ring down over the glued suede; it will be a tight fit and will hold itself in place (diagrams A–C).

3 Repeat Step 2 to secure the other length of suede to the other end of the crystal 'chain' and also to apply the clasp to the other ends of the suede, using the remaining two 4mm jump rings to link the thong to the loops of the clasp.

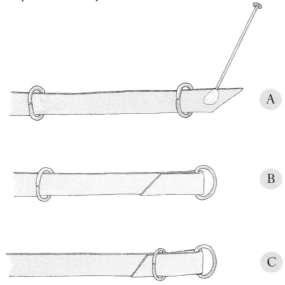

A

B

C

Chunky Charms

—Ease of making: 4
—Time to make: 1½ hours
—Length: 200mm (8in)

This bracelet is another variation on the charm theme and it could be used as a jewellery item to display a selection of your favourite beads or just to use up leftovers from other projects. The beads that I have used are mainly semi-precious stone and many have been surplus to other projects. The charms are silver-plated pewter from a fantastic selection chosen from the pages of one of my favourite American suppliers, Tierracast (see page 126). The item is simple to make and, with different choices of both beads and charms, is infinitely variable.

INGREDIENTS

◎ 10 mixed beads (more if your beads are smaller), 14–22mm
◎ 18 silver-plated pewter charms
◎ 18 'silver' jump rings
◎ 2 sterling silver crimp beads
◎ 2 x 8mm (3/8in) lengths of gimp
◎ 1 silver-plated toggle clasp
◎ 280mm (11in) length of nylon-coated wire.

1 Attach a jump ring to each of the charms, following Steps 4–5 of Making a Thong Necklace, page 18.

2 Make up the bracelet by referring to the photograph for the threading sequence, including the charms, and following the instructions for Simple Necklace Stringing, page 16.

THE CHAIN GANG

Beads and chain are not often used together, but can be a winning combination that allows for styles that would otherwise be impossible. So here I bring you two very different designs to fire your imagination. Chain is available in a wide range of designs and also in precious as well as plated metals, but as a general rule, gold is not often used for beaded jewellery because of its cost.

Celestial Hearts

- Ease of making: 2
- Time to make: 20 minutes
- Length: 110mm (4¼in)

As a jewellery item with appeal, this one has more than most, and many people who have seen these earrings covet them! The drops swing delicately from three varying styles of fine silver chain, and to add an extra dimension, the four 'silver' pendants are all different from each other. Once again, this is a design that can be adapted to suit your requirements, i.e. the chains could be longer, shorter, fewer, more (in quantity) or 'gold' and the pendants could be varied or even just coloured beads. You could also consider making drops such as these to hang as a pendant from a necklace chain or thong.

INGREDIENTS
- ◎ 2 Swarovski crystal heart drops, 10mm
- ◎ 4 different pendants of similar size to the hearts
- ◎ 2 x 80mm (3¼in) lengths of sterling silver chain
- ◎ 2 x 60mm (2½in) lengths of sterling silver chain
- ◎ 2 x 45mm (1¾in) lengths of sterling silver chain
- ◎ 8 sterling silver jump rings, 5mm
- ◎ 2 sterling silver ready-made ear-hooks

1 Attach a jump ring to each of the pendants, following Steps 4–5 of Making a Thong Necklace, page 18. Before closing each jump ring, referring to the photograph for the design, attach each onto the end of a length of chain.

2 Attach the other ends of three matching chains to another jump ring for each earring and then attach these to the ready-made ear-hooks. Finished already!

Opal Hoops

Ease of making: 5
Time to make: 2 hours
Length: 450mm (17¾in)

Sometimes a necklace design just seems to happen while you are wondering what to do with the beads and materials at hand, and this was the case with Opal Hoops. First, I set the 'opals' into the necklace and then intended to form simple straight drops from the links at either side of the set cabochons, but then the idea of looping the threaded rocailles came to mind and this necklace was 'born'! I am very pleased with the unusual style and the flattering way that the necklace sits smooth to the skin.

Although not real, these fake opals are a passable imitation, and the rocailles that I chose to match them also have a pleasing opalescence. However, you could make the same style of necklace in another colourway, as cabochons such as these are available in a wide range of colours in natural stone, glass and acrylic, and to find rocailles to match should be a simple matter.

INGREDIENTS
- 6 cabochons, 10 x 8mm
- 1 x 450mm (17¾in) ready-made chain to take 6 cabochons, 10 x 8mm
- rocailles to match your cabochons
- 12 'silver' crimp beads
- 6 x 180mm (7in) lengths of 'silver' nylon-coated wire
- epoxy glue

1 Lay the chain on a flat surface and check that all your cabochons fit the cup size on the chain. Mix your epoxy glue according to the manufacturer's instructions and apply a small amount (if you use too much it will be squeezed out of the setting when you press the cabochon into place) inside each of the cup settings on the chain, then place a cabochon into each cup. Press into place and then leave to set for the required length of time.

2 When the cabochons are set in place, attach a length of nylon-coated wire to the outside ring at one side of a cabochon cup, following the instructions for Simple Necklace Stringing, page 16, thread on about 40 rocailles and then attach this length of wire to the other ring of the cabochon-set cup (diagram A).

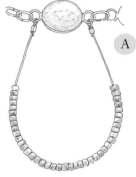

A

3 Repeat Step 2 five more times to complete the necklace.

EARRING FEST

So far a number of earring styles have been covered within various sections, but here, because earrings are always so popular, I show you a whole feast of ear adornments in many different designs. No individual instructions are given, as the techniques to produce them have already been covered.

Earrings really are quite simple to make, but because some people have difficulty mastering the wire-bending technique to make a loop (see Basic Earring Making, page 18), I generally grade them 3 for ease of making.

Flower Power

The very individual lamp glass beads in Flower Power are made by Tuffnell Glass of Yorkshire, England (see page 126), and are available in a wide range of colours. No two will be exactly the same, but as with all handmade glass, I believe this is an appealing trait. The ear-studs are silver plated pewter.

Elegance

These earrings are similar in design to Silver Streak, page 51 , but I have made these to show what difference your choice of findings or colour and size of beads can make to a design.

Damsel Flies

I just love these gorgeous dragonfly pendants and they are super quality with clear enamelled wings that remind me of the blue/green iridescence of the damsel fly. Enamelled pendants such as these are easily available in a wide range of designs. As earrings they are superb, and you will have these made with very little effort or time spent.

Have a Heart

These earrings are one of my personal favourites, so much so that I have a little tale to tell you about them! In any house that I have lived in I have always left a memento hidden for some future resident to find. While writing this book we have had builders working on our house, and recently a hollow beneath the stairs was about to be concreted in, so I found a jar to fit the space and placed into it these earrings and other items. I think it will be centuries before they are found and like to think the finder will get great pleasure from wearing them!

Aztec Charms

Those without pierced ears may be forgiven for thinking that they have been forgotten, as most projects in this book are shown with ear-hooks or -studs, but ear-clips do exist and with very little change to the earring design can be used for most of the projects shown in the book. These particular ear-clips call for a fairly large drop and so to suit them I have used a pendant/necklace end and simply suspended more little pendant drops from it. There are many other styles of ear-clip available.

Spinning Wheels

These earrings are made using the same ear-clip as in Aztec Charms, but a completely different and lighter look is achieved by changing the type of drop and leaving the headpin wire visible as part of the earrings.

In the Pink

The feature beads in this pair of earrings are delicately pretty Bohemian glass with strips of foil beneath a clear pale pink surface. The ear-studs are fine-quality gold-plated pewter.

Rainbow Fluorite Chandeliers

Rainbow fluorite is one of my favourite of the inexpensive natural stones, as it appears in a wide range of tones from green through to purple, and in this pair of earrings I have used beads that exhibit this wide diversity of colour. A few Swarovski crystal beads are also incorporated and they add just a touch of sparkle.

Baby Ninjas

Now for a bit of fun! Many bead suppliers stock little glass animal beads and these are but one example. I think they are cute and I have simply threaded them on an anodized niobium headpin and suspended them from a niobium hoop, as the colour of this material matches the mauve in the bead so perfectly.

MONEY EARNERS

If, after sampling the projects in this book, you are fired with enthusiasm for beading and you would like to make it more than a hobby by selling your jewellery, where do you start? Or maybe your local school or community has a summer or Christmas fête in the offing and you would like to help raise funds, but how do you begin? This section gives you a few ideas for starter items that can be made with little expense but could be sold at a good profit. And for those with children there are also one or two that they would enjoy helping with.

Perhaps you want to turn your hobby into a serious profit-making business, in which case you need to consider the various sales methods and venues available and select those that suit you best, whether selling to shops or on the Internet, or through a party plan or at craft fairs.

Golf Score Counter

This counter, which works by sliding beads on crossed cord, can be made very cheaply by using inexpensive plastic beads, as in the blue example shown, or you could make more upmarket versions by employing better-quality components, as in the other score counter, which is made from various semi-precious stone beads. Obviously, if you are selling the latter, you must take the cost of the materials into account and mark your price up accordingly.

Making a golf score counter such as this is easy and it is a project that quite young children could help with, although they would need adult supervision and assistance when fixing the square calotte crimp to the cord and the key ring.

INGREDIENTS ◎ 10 large-holed beads of the same size ◎ 1 'silver' jump ring ◎ 1 square calotte crimp ◎ 1 key ring without chain ◎ 500mm (20in) length of 1mm cotton cord (this length will suit beads of about 8–10mm diameter)

1 Thread one bead onto the centre of the cotton cord, then thread on one more bead and thread the other side of the cotton cord back through the second bead. Thread on another bead and again thread the other side of the cotton cord back through this bead (diagram A).

2 Continue threading beads on as in Step 1 until you have threaded ten beads. Apply a square calotte crimp to encase both ends of the cord together and use the jump ring to attach the finished item to the key ring, following the instructions for Making a Thong Necklace, page 18. Now give this to the golfer in your life and hope that they won't be offended by the number of beads!

A

Selling to shops

This is often on a 'sale or return' basis, so you won't be paid up front, but it does enable you to control the stock, removing any that is out of season or not selling. You will need to negotiate the percentage of sales revenue that the shop will take and who covers the cost of stolen property (usually the shop proprietor). Remember that your selling price will need to cover the shop's share of the profits. Keep accurate records of the stock they hold.

Elephant Bracelet

This is a great item for selling at a school fête, as it is sure to appeal to young children who may have a little money to spend. It is extremely inexpensive to make, so when offered for sale, the mark-up potential is good. Animal beads such as these are available in a wide range of colours and type of animal, and they cost very little. Once more, this is a project that young children could help with, although, as before, they would need supervision and assistance with applying the square calotte crimps.

INGREDIENTS ◎ 1 animal bead ◎ 2 square calotte crimps ◎ 1 hook clasp ◎ 250mm (10in) length of rainbow rat-tail

To make up the bracelet, refer to the photograph for the design and follow the instructions for Making a Thong Necklace, page 18, making a simple overhand knot in the rat-tail either side of the animal bead.

Specialist Jewellery

If you find yourself really drawn to one type of jewellery or materials, such as pearls, consider becoming a specialist maker/seller in that field, for instance, in the case of pearls, in bridal jewellery. Establish a name for yourself by advertising in appropriate magazines or newspapers or by taking a stand at bridal fairs.

Selling to the Public

If you are confident and enjoy dealing with people, why not try selling your jewellery through a party plan? Because most women like jewellery and many of the items are inexpensive, you should have little difficulty finding people willing to host the parties or party guests to attend them, and the profits are good. Attend and host a few parties yourself first to see how it works. Or, take a stand at a craft fair. Start small and find out what sells before investing in a costly stand at a large venue.

Simple Earrings

Simple earrings can be very inexpensive to make and as jewellery items appeal to all ages, so here I give several examples made using cheaper beads and plated metal components. The project is not suitable for young children, but dexterous older children should be able to cope quite well. My daughter, for instance, was quite competent at making earrings such as these by the age of ten; however, you should judge this for yourself and supervise early attempts!

INGREDIENTS ◎ selection of mixed beads in matched pairs for threading onto the headpins ◎ 2 plated metal headpins, 50mm ◎ 2 plated metal ready-made ear-hooks

To make up the earrings, refer to the photographs and follow the instructions for Basic Earring Making, page 18.

Bright and Beautiful

Probably the simplest project in the book, these bracelets are strung on a material not shown in any other section. It is Stretch Magic and, as its name suggests, is stretchy; just what the magic is I am not sure, but maybe it refers to the fact that once a knot is tied in this 'thread', it stays put and does not easily come undone! The beads, which are made from glass, are available in a wide colour range and are very inexpensive; for just a few pounds Sterling you will get about 250. This means that at today's prices the bracelet costs about 30 pence (50 cents) to make!

INGREDIENTS ◎ 22 crackle glass beads, 8mm ◎ 450mm (17¾in) length of Stretch Magic ◎ flexible twisted wire beading needle

Simply thread your needle with the Stretch Magic and thread on the beads until the bracelet is the required size, then tie the two ends of the Stretch Magic together in a knot to finish.

Cord Chokers

The choker necklace is one of the most versatile styles of simple jewellery and on a length of cord, suede, ribbon or leather thong you can thread a few beads to make an item to appeal to anyone, from toddler to grandmother. A bag of mixed or old beads could provide materials for a great many necklaces. Just follow the instructions for Making a Thong Necklace, page 18.

Memory Wire Bracelets

Memory wire is a great material on which to base a bracelet and as a jewellery item for children it is perfect, as there are no fiddly clasps with which little ones have to fumble. It is also virtually indestructible. However, it is not advisable to let young children attempt this as a project, as the unfinished ends of memory wire are very sharp and springy and can catch on delicate skin.

The beads that I have used here are wooden and are available in a wide range of bright colours and other sizes and shapes, but many other types of inexpensive bead would be suitable for this project.

INGREDIENTS ◎ 11 coloured wooden beads (or your own selection of beads), 12 x 5mm ◎ 12 coloured wooden beads, 4mm ◎ 2 metal beads, 3mm ◎ 1 bracelet length of memory wire

Refer to the photograph for the threading sequence (the first and last beads to be threaded are the 3mm metal beads to stop the other beads sliding over the ends of the wire) and follow the instructions for Bunny Bangle, page 91, for using memory wire.

GLOSSARY

AB-coating
Short for aurora borealis, AB refers to a surface coating applied to some beads to give a special iridescent finish.

Bail
Metal component to thread onto necklace or cord from which to suspend a pendant.

Bead Caps
Metal cup-shaped component of very variable size to fit close to and 'cup' a bead as part of the jewellery design.

Beaded Rondel
Metal bead often used as a spacer between other beads, 'beaded' refers to its appearance of having small beads around its outside edge.

Beading Tray
Purpose-made tray with moulded necklace grooves to help with design and also with depressed sections to hold beads while working.

Bicone Beads
Beads that are cone shaped at both ends.

Calottes
Metal component usually used as a necklace end. Many are cup shaped to hold and hide the end knot of a necklace. They have a loop for attaching to a clasp.

Channel Set
A method of setting stones in which the metal wire that holds a jewellery 'stone' is 'V'-shaped in cross section and the edge of the 'stone' sits inside the 'V'.

Clutch-back
The fitting that slides onto the post of an ear-stud to hold it in place in the ear.

Crimp Bead
A type of metal bead that is made to be squeezed with pliers so that it presses down onto a threading medium to secure it in place, often used together with nylon-coated wire to make attachments to clasps.

Ear-clip
An ear-fitting that is worn by clipping to the ear with an in-built spring-type fastening.

Ear-hook
An ear-fitting that is worn by hooking through the ear.

Ear-stud (or Ear-post)
An ear-fitting that has a straight 'post' that fits through the ear and is secured by a clutch-back (see below).

Enamel
Coloured glass fused to the surface of metal by the application of heat.

Feature or Focal Bead/s
The main bead or beads in an item of jewellery.

Findings
The general term given to all metal components used in jewellery making.

Flat Washer Bead
A plain rondel.

Flexible Twisted Wire Beading Needle
A fine pliable needle made from a twisted length of very strong wire, particularly useful for threading beads with fine holes.

Frosted Glass
A finish given to glass beads by tumbling in abrasive grits or by etching with acid.

Gel Superglue
Cyanoacrylate glue in gel form, useful for sealing knots and other jewellery gluing jobs, but be careful not to get it on beads, otherwise they will be spoilt, or to get it on yourself!

Hatpin
A long pointed pin (similar to a headpin) used for threading beads to make a decorative beaded hatpin.

Headpin
Metal pins (like small extremely fine long nails) used for threading beads onto to make earring drops.

Heishi
Small metal tube-shaped beads.

Gimp
Open very flexible coils of extremely fine wire used for threading through and hiding the thread at the ends of necklaces.

Goldfill
Metal finish of real gold bonded to a less-expensive metal.

Jump Rings
Circles of wire used for joining one component to another.

Lamp Beads
Handmade glass beads formed with the heat of a lamp.

Memory Wire
A hard springy sort of wire that is made in continuous coils, from which lengths are cut to form the base of necklaces, bracelets and rings. It has the unusual property of returning to its original shape after being pulled apart.

Millefiori
Literally means 'a thousand flowers' and refers to a type of floral decoration invented by the Venetian glass artists of old.

Monofilament Nylon Beading Thread
Single-thread clear nylon, just like fishing line!

Necklace End Cap
Metal bell-shaped finding used at either ends of a necklace to conceal end beads, crimp beads or thread.

Nylon-coated Wire
A type of wire that beneath a smooth (often coloured) nylon surface conceals multiple strands of wire. Extremely useful in beaded jewellery making.

Pliers
Gripping and cutting tools used to assist with cutting and bending wire (see page 14).

Rat-tail
A cord with a silky finish, which is available in a huge range of attractive colours.

Spacer Bars
Used in necklaces and earrings to separate the beaded strings in multi-strand jewellery.

Square Calotte Crimp
A metal finding usually used as a thong necklace end that secures the thong to the clasp.

Stretch Magic
A stretchy threading medium.

Teardrop Bead
A pear-shaped bead.

Trade Bead
A bead used in the past for trade purposes and exchange of goods.

ACKNOWLEDGMENTS

First and foremost, my deep appreciation goes to my husband David who has patiently proof-read and re-read these pages, and taken over all housework duties and gardening while I have been glued to the computer. Thanks also to my children, who have now flown the nest, but continue to be interested in and encourage my beading activities; Andrew for the odd word or two of computer advice and Theresa who, with youthful enthusiasm, has started her own bead business and ensured that I stay abreast of modern trends. Also, and I'm not sure whether to thank them or not, but I must mention our builders who have, as quietly as possible, gone about the business of extending our house around me and the beads.

Most of the beads and findings used for the projects in the book were supplied by the following companies and individuals, and I would like to thank them for their wonderful products and their cooperation.

Burhouse Ltd
Quarmby Mills
Tanyard Road, Oakes
Huddersfield HD3 4YP, UK
tel: 00 44 1484 655 675
www.burhouse.com
Suppliers of findings and natural stone beads and other products.

Creative Beadcraft Ltd
Unit 2 Asheridge Business Centre
Asheridge Road, Chesham
Buckinghamshire HP5 2PT, UK
tel: 00 44 1494 778 818
www.creativebeadcraft.co.uk
Suppliers of beads, findings and storage, etc.

Dora Schubert
Gatzer Ring 3b, 21465 Wentorf
Germany
www.doraschubert.com
Glass bead manufacturer.

Jewelex Collection
Suite 325, 2005 Merrick Road
NY 11566, USA
tel: 001 516 771 9473
www.jewelex.com
Stockists of vintage glass beads and metal findings.

JRM Beads Ltd
16 Redbridge Enterprise Centre
Thompson Close, Ilford
Essex IG1 1TY, UK
tel: 0044 20 8553 3240
www.beadworks.co.uk
Mail order company selling a wide range of beads, findings and storage, etc.

Klews Expressions
(see opposite)
435 West J Street
Tehachapi CA 93561, USA
tel: 001 661 823 1930
www.klewexpressions.com
Manufacturer of polymer clay beads.

Mineral Warehouse
Vale Craft Studios, Findon Road
Findon, Worthing
West Sussex BN14 0RA, UK
tel: 00 44 1903 877 037
www.minware.co.uk
Suppliers of all types of natural stone beads and other products.

Reactive Metals Studio
PO Box 890
600 First North Street,
Clarkdale AZ8634, USA
tel: 001 928 634 3434
www.reactivemetals.com
Manufacturers of goldfill and sterling silver beads and findings, and niobium products.

Tierracast
3177 Guerneville Road
Santa Rosa CA 95401, USA
tel: 001 503 678 2926 or
001 707 545 5787
www.tierracast.com
Manufacturers of cast gold and silver-plated pewter findings, beads, connectors and pendants.

Tuffnell Glass
38 Wansford Road, Driffield
East Yorkshire, YO25 5NF, UK
tel: 00 44 1377 240 745
www.tuffnellglass.co.uk
Glass bead manufacturers.

Kits for the projects featured in this book, as well as other loose beads, findings and ready-made jewellery, can be obtained from my daughter Theresa Case:

BeauJangles
Higher Loady Park Farm
Whitehill Road, Highweek,
Newton Abbot
Devon TQ12 1QE, UK
tel: 0044 1626 777 226
mobile: 07790 262875

Bead Supply Companies

I have tried to include every UK bead supplier that I know of, but apologies to those who have been missed. For all others I have had to rely on Internet searches, so please forgive me if you have been missed!

UK

Bead Exclusive
Nixon House
Teignmouth Road
Torquay
Devon TQ1 4HA
tel: 0044 1803 322 000
www.beadexclusive.com

Beadgems
www.beadgems.com

Earring Things
Craft Workshops
South Pier Road
Ellesmere Port
Cheshire CH65 4FW
tel: 0044 1513 564 444
www.beadmaster.com

GJ Beads
Units 1–3 Court Arcade
The Wharf, St Ives
Cornwall TR26 1LG
tel: 0044 1736 793 886
www.gjbeads.co.uk

Glass with Class
Dept PPC
20 Mendip Walk
West Green, Crawley
West Sussex RH11 7JZ
tel: 0044 1293 417 035

Jilly Beads
29 Hexham Road
Morecombe LA4 6PE
tel: 0044 1524 412 728
www.jillybeads.com

Kernowcraft Rocks & Gems Ltd
Bolingcy
Perranporth
Cornwall TR6 0DH
tel: 0044 1872 573 888
www.kernowcraft.com

Manchester Minerals
Georges Road, Stockport
Cheshire SK4 1DP
tel: 0044 1614 805 095
email: gemcraft@btconnect.com

The Rocking Rabbit Trading Company
226a High Street, Cottenham
Cambridge CB4 8RZ
tel: 0044 8706 061 588
www.rockingrabbit.co.uk

Spangles
1 Casburn Lane, Burwell
Cambridge CB5 0ED
www.spangles4beads.co.uk

USA

Bangles and Beads
3322 West Cary Street
Richmond VA 232211
www.banglesandbeads.net

Bead Bar
1319 Edgewater Drive
Orlando FL 32804
tel: 001 407 426 8826
www.beadbar.com

Bead Boppers
394 S Meridian
Puyallup WA 98373
tel: 001 253 848 3880

Beadiak
3815 A East Thousand Oaks Blvd
Thousand Oaks CA 91362
tel: 001 805 497 8083

Beading Frenzy
333 E Fourth Avenue
San Mateo CA 94401
tel: 001 650 347 BEAD

Beadworks
167 Newbury Street
Boston MA 02116
tel: 001 617 247 7227
www.beadworks.com

Beadworks
23 Church Street
Cambridge MA 02138
tel: 001 617 868 9777
www.beadworks.com

Beadworks
139 Washington Street
South Norwalk CT 06854
tel: 001 203 852 9194
www.beadworks.com

Beadworks
149 Water Street
Norwalk CT 06854
tel: 001 203 852 9108
www.beadworks.com

Beadworks
602 South 2nd Street
Philadelphia PA 19147
tel: 001 215 413 2323
www.beadworks.com

Beadworks
290 Thayer Street
Providence RI 02906
tel: 001 401 861 4540
www.beadworks.com

Beadworks
7632 Campbell Road
Dallas TX 75248
tel: 001 972 931 4540
www.beadworks.com

Bella Beads
395 North State Street
Lake Oswengo OR 97034
tel: 001 503 635 2073
www.bellabeads-shop.com

Bourget Jewelcraft Supplies
1636 BB 11th Street
Santa Monica CA 90404
tel: 001 800 828 3024

Buttons, Bangles and Beads
415 Corey Avenue
St Pete Beach FL 33706
tel: 001 727 363 4332
www.buttonsbanglesandbeads.com

Helby Import
1501 South Park Avenue
Linden NJ 07036
tel: 001 732 969 5300
www.helby.com

Klews Expressions
104 W Panamint Avenue
Ridgecrest CA 93555
tel: 001 760 384 BEAD
www.klewexpressions.com

Oriental Treasures Inc
Bellevue Center Mall
7620 Highway, 70 S Suite 108
Nashville TN 37221
tel: 001 615 646 5383
www.look4beads.com

Shipwreck Beads
8560 Commerce Place Drive
NE Lacey WA 98516
tel: 001 360 754 2323
www.shipwreckbeads.com

WildAboutBeads.com
436 Main Road
Tiverton RI 02878-1314
tel: 001 401 624 4332
www.wildaboutbeads.com

Canada

Austin Hamilton Studio
3825 Henning Drive
Suite 115, Buraby
British Columbia
V5C 6P3
tel. 001 604 291 8113
www.ah.minek.com

Bead Closet
8118–103 Edmonton Street
Alberta T6E 4B1
tel: 001 780 732 7547
www.beadcloset.com

Beadworks
126 West 3rd Avenue
Vancouver BC V51E9
tel: 001 604 876 6637
www.beadworks.com

Designer Beads
101 Gorevale Avenue
Toronto, Ontario
M6J 2R5
www.designerbeads.com

That Bead Lady
390 Davis Drive
Newmarket, Ontario
L3Y 7T8
tel: 001 905 954 1327
www.thatbeadlady.com

Germany

Gems 2 Behold
Im Grund 18
36304, Alsfeld
tel: 0049 845 280 1667
www.gems2behold.com

France

Bead-e
3258 route de Vaudagne
74310 Les Houches
tel: 0033 450 914 034
www.bead-e.com

Le Comptoir Des Perles
21 bis, rue d'Hennemont
78100 Saint Germain en-Laye
tel: 0033 130 870 808

Japan

Beadworks
www.beadworks.jp

Australia

The Bead Bar
Shop 3 Metcalfe Avenue
80 George Street
The Rocks NSW 2000
tel: 0061 292 475 946
www.thebeadbar.com.au

The Bead Company of
Australia *stores in various locations*
Sydney Store
1/22 Brigantine Street
Sydney
tel: 0061 295 571 228
www.beadcompany.com.au

The Bead Shop
PO Box 1792
Byron Bay NSW 2481
tel: 0061 266 858 994
www.thebeadshop.com

Beadhouse and Casting
4 Stikes Avenue, Alexandria
Sydney NSW 2015
tel: 0061 293 193 335
www.beadhouse.com.au

Beadzone
Shop 157
Westfield Whitford City
Hillarys WA 6025
tel: 0061 930 72811
www.beadzone.com.au

Crystal Flair
PO Box 99
Wickham WA 6720
tel: 0061 891 871 888
www.crystalflair.com.au

Ebeads Direct
PO Box 1172
Toowong 4066
Brisbane, Queensland
tel: 0061 410 399445
www.ebeadsdirect.com

Not Just Beadz
PO Box 358
Drummoyne
Sydney NSW 20477
www.notjustbeadz.com.au

Spacetrader Beads
PO Box 1019
St Kilda South, Melbourne
Victoria 3182
tel: 0061 395 346 867
www.spacetrader.com.au

Unique Beads
PO Box 246
Thornlie WA 6988
www.uniquebeads.com.au

New Zealand

Beadz Unlimited
Wellington and Christchurch
www.beadzunlimited.co.nz

Ebeads Direct
PO Box 6448, Dunedin
tel: 0064 274 546 912
www.ebeadsdirect.com

INDEX

About the Author

For over 30 years, a fascination with beads has led Barbara Case on an exciting path, from simple re-stringing to establishing a large successful mail order business and designing for country-wide retail stores. In recent years Barbara has sold the business, but continues to keep abreast of everything new in beading, and still designs and makes beautiful jewellery. She is the author of the best-selling *Making Beaded Jewellery*, also published by David & Charles.

If you have any queries or need advice about the projects or beads within this book, please contact the author by post or email:

Barbara Case
Wren House, 27 Manor Road, Bishopsteignton,
Devon, TQ14 9SU, United Kingdom

email: bd.thornton@onetel.net